PAVLOVA

PAVLOVA

Repertoire of a Legend

John and Roberta Lazzarini

A Dance Horizons Book

SCHIRMER BOOKS
A Division of Macmillan Publishing Co., Inc.
NEW YORK

Collier Macmillan Publishers
LONDON

Frontispiece, page 2: Studio portrait by Boissonnas & Eggler, St. Petersburg, 1903.

Part title photo, page 23: As Zulme in *Giselle*. Photograph by Boissonnas & Eggler, St. Petersburg, 1899.

Part title photo, page 127: *Night*. Photograph by Saul Bransburg. London, 1912.

End photo, page 224: In the *grand pas classique* from *Paquita*. Photograph by Yaravoff, Montevideo, 1928.

Copyright © 1980 by John and Roberta Lazzarini

SCHIRMER BOOKS
A Division of Macmillan Publishing Co., Inc.
866 Third Avenue, New York, N.Y. 10022

Collier Macmillan Canada, Ltd.

Library of Congress Catalog Card Number: 80-5560

Printed in the United States of America

printing number

1 2 3 4 5 6 7 8 9 10

Library of Congress Cataloging in Publication Data

Lazzarini, John.
  Pavlova: repertoire of a legend.

  Includes index.
  1. Pavlova, Anna, 1881–1931. 2. Ballet dancers—
Russia—Biography. I. Lazzarini, Roberta, joint author.
GV1785.P3L39   792.8′092′4 [B]   80-5560
ISBN 0-02-871970-0

Designed by John and Roberta Lazzarini

To
Dame Alicia Markova
and to the memory of
Manya Charchevnikova

Contents

Part Two: 1912–1930

Posing for the press in the garden at Ivy House, in costume for *Chopiniana.* Photograph, 1924.

Preface

The prime force in Pavlova's life was her art. She always insisted that only the time when she appeared on stage was real, that the routine, everyday occurrences of life were "a mirage." And although experts disagree about the greatest influences in her life and the time when she reached her peak, although they argue for and against the worth of her repertoire, all are of one accord when it comes to what to her was most important—performance. In that, they agree, she was "incomparable."

This book is devoted to Pavlova in performance, documenting her vast repertoire and picturing her in some ninety of her roles. In arranging the material we have generally followed the chronology of the photographs rather than the chronology of first performance. In this way readers may gain a clearer idea of the evolution of Pavlova's artistry and of the progress of a life virtually spent on the stages of the world.

The body of the book is divided into two parts. In Part One (1892–1911) we trace Pavlova's development, from a talented, faltering beginner to prima ballerina, in a series of short essays based on descriptions and impressions from contemporary sources. Part Two (1912–1930) is purely documentary; following brief statements of data pertinent to Pavlova's roles are extracts from press notices of her performances around the world.

Throughout the book, our only intrusions in quotations have been to clarify occasionally erratic punctuation and to simplify some spellings of names translated or transliterated from foreign languages. Russian names are spelled according to their most common usage. Russian dates are given in the Old Style, by the Julian calendar. For corresponding dates in the Western, or Gregorian, calendar, add twelve days in the nineteenth century and thirteen days in the twentieth.

As well as creating an informative book of interest to the general reader, we have endeavored to provide a valuable reference work for the dance scholar. To this end we have included a section of detailed notes at the back of the book, where readers will also find a bibliography and a chronological list of Pavlova's repertoire. In selecting illustrations we have singled out those of historical and documentary value, and we have taken considerable pains to identify photographers and to date the photographs.

We hope that this book will not only celebrate Pavlova's centennial year but that it will inspire a more profound awareness of the remarkable woman who in the early part of this century became the most famous ballerina in the world, and who remains a perpetual inspiration for dancers everywhere.

Acknowledgments

To all who, throughout the world, have given their advice, friendship, skill, and patience so unstintingly in the course of this book's creation: we thank you.

Dr. Vera Krasovskaya—dance historian and our treasured friend in Leningrad—has given us constant encouragement and the benefit of her profound knowledge of Pavlova's career and the history of the Russian ballet. Without her generous help, this book could not have existed. Beverley Gallegos, in New York, has been our tireless researcher and warm host. Closer to home, Jennie Walton has given consistent help, enthusiasm, and inspiration. Leonard Newman and Anna Way have pursued the story of Pavlova with us in the archives of the world's press, with dedication and unflagging zeal. Leonard Newman documented the contents of the *Annual of the Imperial Theaters* in the British Library, Bloomsbury.

Anna Pavlova's career was international. Our record of it could not have been achieved without the support and wisdom of a worldwide community of people and organizations. We remember with gratitude the many friends who, in the course of our twenty journeys to Leningrad and Moscow, guided us to rare and invaluable source material relating to Pavlova's career at the Maryinsky Theater. For help in dealing with this material we thank our team of translators, Lesley Clifford, Margaret Dodds, Anita von Etzdorf, Gabriele Rothardt, and Jean Tongue, who also gathered other records of the story from French, German, Polish, and Spanish sources.

Well beyond the call of duty were the efforts of Peter Davies, who while working for the British Council in India generously undertook to research Pavlova's work with Uday Shankar. Still farther eastward, Kenji Usui of Osaka provided us with invaluable documentation of Pavlova's visit to Japan.

If we cannot list the host of students and friends of Pavlova throughout the world whom we have pursued with our inquiries for so long, they will forgive us. Of those, however, whose assistance proved indispensable we thank Donald Abram, David Bard, Jacques Baril, Keith Barrett, John Bellingham, Ivan Best, Alan and Marilyn Brien, Judy Cameron, Jasmin Cannon Bell, Renato Casellato, Eileen Condell, Anne Dodds, Anton Dolin, Margot Ettlinger, Francesca Franchi, Richard Holland, Victoria Huckenpahler, Marjorie Lucas, Nesta Macdonald, Peter Moldon, Robert Monroe, Mildred Prause, Nadia Nerina, Stella Paine, Frances Pritchard, Jane Pritchard, Mary Pritchard, Claire Robilant, Estelle and Lionel Russell, Arthur Samuel, Jennie Schulman, Boris Skidelsky, Anna Taylor, Peter Way, Philip Whichelo, and Barry Willoughby.

To Dame Margot Fonteyn and to former members of the Pavlova company Juliet Gervis, Rita Glynde, Stanley Judson, Molly Lake, Cléo Nordi, and Muriel Stuart we are deeply indebted. To Harry Mills, a former manager of Pavlova's company and widower of her beloved Hilda Butsova, we owe particular thanks.

We must pay special tribute to Dame Marie Rambert, Dame Ninette de Valois, Sir Frederick Ashton, and Arnold Haskell, all of whom knew Pavlova and fell under her spell. These four pioneers of British ballet have kindly allowed us to quote from conversations and lectures over the years, when Pavlova was the subject of discussion.

Dance scholars Ivor Guest and David Vaughan gave us valuable help, as did Reynaldo Alejandro and Lacy McDearmon of the Dance Collection at the Library and Museum of the Performing Arts, Lincoln Center. John O'Brien we sincerely thank for his wholehearted support during the preparation of this book and for the many opportunities he afforded us to study at leisure his meticulously chronicled collection of ballet material, and in particular for the loan of his very rare photograph of Pavlova in *Christmas* by Baron de Meyer.

We acknowledge with equal gratitude the cooperation of the following institutions: the Bolshoi Theater Museum, Moscow; the Bakhrushin Theater Museum, Moscow; the State Archive of Ballet Theater, Moscow; the Central State Historical Archive, Leningrad; the Leningrad State Institute of Theater, Music, and Cinematography; the Leningrad State Theater Museum; the Museum of the Vaganova Choreographic School, Leningrad; the British Library, Bloomsbury; the Newspaper Library, Colindale; the Theatre Museum, London; the Museum of London; the Deutsches Staatsbibliothek, Berlin; the Bibliothèque de l'Opéra, Paris; the Bibliothèque de l'Arsenal, Paris; the New York Public Library; the Theatre and Music Collection of the Museum of the City of New York; the Special Collections Division of the University of Washington Libraries in Seattle; the Verdak Collection, Indianapolis; the Library of New South Wales, Mitchell Library, Sydney; and the City of Mildura Arts Center.

The creation of this book has not been without incident. We have been sustained from the outset by the members of the Pavlova Society and in particular by Pamela Gray, Michael Dickens, and Colin Cushway Jones. Our greatest joy has been our collaboration with Claude Conyers, that most sensitive of editors, who has so willingly given us his expert advice and friendly support. Our greatest sorrow is that Tamara Karsavina, who helped us so much, did not live to see the book's publication.

R. L. & J. L.
August 1980

Biographical Sketch

Anna Pavlova was born in St. Petersburg on January 31, 1881. Her life's ambition crystallized in childhood, at a performance of *The Sleeping Beauty* at the Maryinsky Theater. "It never entered my mind," she remembered later, "that there were easier goals to attain than that of principal dancer of the Imperial Ballet." In 1891 she was admitted to the famous ballet academy on Theater Street.

Pavlova soon attracted attention from her teachers, who singled her out for her exceptional musicality and curtailed her misguided attempts to emulate the pyrotechnics of the Italian ballerinas then in vogue at the Maryinsky. In academic subjects she excelled, but it was not until her last two years at the school that her dancing talent asserted itself. Her first important role was in *The Two Stars*, revived by Marius Petipa for the school performance at the Mikhailovsky Theater on March 29, 1898. On April 11 of the following year she gave her graduation performance at the same theater, dancing in two ballets, Pavel Gerdt's *Imaginary Dryads* and Alexander Gorsky's *Clorinda*.

Bypassing the *corps de ballet*, Pavlova was accepted into the Maryinsky company in 1899. In 1902 her reputation was firmly established with her performances as Nikiya in Petipa's *La Bayadère*. Pavlova had by then developed a genuine affection for the aging ballet master, who was by no means her only ally. She was surrounded by a friendly army of influential and wealthy people, not least of whom was Victor Dandré, an aristocratic balletomane who had followed her career from her schooldays. Pavlova was thus well equipped to survive and flourish in the world of intrigue behind the façade of the Maryinsky Theater.

And flourish she did, soon extending her popularity to other theaters and other cities. In 1904 Pavlova traveled to Moscow, where she danced for the first time at the Bolshoi Theater, and to Warsaw, where she was acclaimed for her interpretation of Giselle at the Wielki Theater. Yet, in the dancers' strike of 1905 Pavlova was prepared to risk her burgeoning career in a militant role against the Maryinsky management. In spite of this, she was officially appointed to the rank of prima ballerina the following year. Her performances were so popular that students would apply for jobs as extras just to see them. Theater staff would crowd into the auditorium to watch her rehearsals. Such was her prestige that in the spring of 1907 she was granted her first independent tour and with Michel Fokine led a small company of dancers to Moscow, where she performed the leading roles in many ballets for the first time. As well as excelling in classical roles, Pavlova adapted herself beautifully to the free-flowing movements demanded by Fokine's choreography. The short solo *The Swan*, created for her by Fokine in the same year, was to become indelibly identified with her name in the popular imagination.

Pavlova's international fame was established in 1908, when with Adolph Bolm she led a small touring group from the Maryinsky to Helsingfors (Helsinki), Copenhagen, Stockholm, Berlin, Dresden, Leipzig, and a number of small towns. Her success was repeated in other European cities the following year, this time with Nicolas Legat. As leading ballerina of the touring company, she danced several important roles denied her at the Maryinsky. After her 1909 tour she traveled immediately to Paris to appear in Diaghilev's Saison Russe, but she felt restricted by the repertoire, complaining that in Paris "they served up Russian art like Russian food—too luxuriously and too copiously."

Her rapturous reception in the European capitals doubtless contributed to Pavlova's decision to resign from the Maryinsky in 1910, the year of her first triumphant seasons in New York and London. Furthermore, upon her return to St. Petersburg from America in 1911, she found herself involved in a scandal that was to change her life. Victor Dandré, a member of St. Petersburg's City Council, had been arrested on a charge of appropriating vast sums of government money. Upon Pavlova's arrival he was released on bail, after having promised not to leave the city. Within a few weeks both Dandré and Pavlova were in London. She subsequently revisited Russia, but he was never to return, and Pavlova's loyalty to him committed her to life outside her homeland.

In 1912 Pavlova and Dandré settled permanently in London, taking up residence in Ivy House, Golders Green, which they purchased in 1914. This was to be the base for Pavlova's world tours. Gathering a small company around her, she traveled extensively and continuously, presenting ballet in major capitals of the world as well as remote towns and villages, dancing anywhere there was a stage and in many places where there was none. The administration of her company and the complex arrangement of her vast touring schedule was masterminded by Dandré, a brilliant organizer, who always remained in the background. Although their relationship was never clearly defined, he was a protagonist in the story of Pavlova's life, and he cannot be lightly dismissed as a minor figure.

Two decades of exhaustive and exhausting touring finally took their toll. In January 1931, returning from a short holiday in Cannes, Pavlova caught a chill en route to Paris, where rehearsals were to begin for her forthcoming tour. By the time she reached Holland, the starting point of the tour, she had developed pneumonia. She died in a bedroom of the Hôtel des Indes in The Hague in the early hours of January 23, 1931.

In *The Swan*. Studio photograph by Jean de Strelecki, New York, c. 1914. This was Pavlova's favorite image of herself. She had it reproduced on posters, playbills, and souvenir programs all over the world.

Images of Pavlova

Pavlova was one of the most photographed women of her time. An extraordinary number of photographic studies have survived, including depictions of almost all the roles in her repertoire. From 1892, during her student days in Russia, through 1930, when she made her last provincial tour of Britain, hundreds of photographs were made at various times and places under diverse conditions.

Despite the richness of this material, the image of Pavlova as an artist that continues to flourish in the public mind is a stilted and unbalanced one. The all too familiar studies of her (usually as the Swan), highly stylized and heavily retouched, conceal almost more than they reveal. She who slipped so quickly into the realm of legend seems to have little more substance than the lithographic images of dancers of more than a century ago. Pavlova herself is partly to blame. Throughout her life she remained steadfast in her decided preference for highly stylized and heavily retouched photographs. Thus, the general public's view of her can hardly be ascribed only to the technical limitations of photography at the turn of the century.

At that time, dancers, like everyone else who faced a camera, had to observe strict conventions. Periods of exposure were painfully long; for several seconds the subject had to remain completely motionless. For this reason dancers were usually photographed standing with both feet placed firmly on the floor. Otherwise, they might be posed sitting, kneeling, or in a reclining attitude, often with the head resting on a supporting arm. On the rare occasions when a dancer was photographed in a pose simulating action, the body was held in position by wooden supports that enabled the subject to maintain the pose for whatever length of time the camera demanded. After the negative plates were developed, the photographer would painstakingly remove all evidence of supporting devices before printing the finished picture.

The more important St. Petersburg studios, such as Fischer and Boissonnas & Eggler, exercised considerable artistic license. Picturesque backdrops, mirrors, and other props were employed to enhance the atmosphere of each study. The practice of photographing a subject in a series of costumes and poses from different ballets but in front of the same "artistic" backdrop was to present problems of identification to later ballet scholars. Nevertheless, photographs made in these two studios were artistic creations in their own right.

Interesting studies were also made in the Maryinsky Theater's own private photographic studio, particularly to record such important occasions as galas, benefits, and jubilees. Artists of the Maryinsky posed for official portraits as well as in costume for their roles, and many photographs of them were published in the *Annual of the Imperial Theaters*, a lavishly illustrated yearbook that documented performances of opera, ballet, and drama. The Office of the Imperial Theaters also customarily issued postcard photographs of its artists (see pages 38–39). The balletomanes, who were a prominent, exclusive, and highly organized section of St. Petersburg society, would campaign for postcards of their favorite dancers by bombarding the theater administration with innumerable requests. It is largely thanks to their enthusiasm and to the craft of the St. Petersburg studios that so many early photographs of Pavlova survive to the present day.

Among Pavlova's outstanding qualities that were rarely captured by the camera were her elevation and the remarkable impression that she gave of flight. From most photographs of her one inevitably forms the idea that she was a *terre à terre* dancer, when in fact the opposite was true. Attempts to express her aerial quality were, however, occasionally made. The St. Petersburg photographers experimented with artistically arranged gauzes and veils, and during Pavlova's first tours abroad in 1908 and 1909, many quite pleasing studies of the ballerina "on point" were made by the Berlin studios (notably that of Schneider). But these were essentially static (see page 87) and were merely extensions of what had been done before. Only the studio of Zander & Labisch, in a remarkable study of *Swan Lake* (see page 92), was successfully able to convey the image of flight that Pavlova projected.

In 1909, during Diaghilev's Saison Russe in Paris, Pavlova posed for a series of photographs before a crumpled curtain serving as a backdrop. Primarily concerned with capturing a surface record, the photographer, Bert, made no attempt at creating any artistic image whatsoever (see pages 98–103). Although these photographs were to become historically invaluable, they were in their own time nothing but a retrograde step in ballet photography.

The following year a remarkable series was produced by the New York studios of Herman Mishkin (see pages 114–117). These pictures of Pavlova and Mikhail Mordkin in *Bacchanale* have a freeze-frame quality and at last convey a sense of the dynamic movement of the dance. A few months later this development was even further refined. England's Dover Street Studios produced a stunning set of photographs of *Valse Caprice* (see pages 111–113). These subtlest and most sophisticated of ballet studies capture the spontaneity of the action shots that were yet to come.

Prior to World War I and her departure for America, Pavlova was constantly in demand by London's leading photographers. The illustrated weeklies made exclusive studies of her, for which she posed under every sort of condition, often in the open air. Photographs taken in

In Dance of the Ural Cossacks in *The Humpbacked Horse*. Photographed in Fischer's studio, St. Petersburg, shortly after her debut in this role on October 27, 1902. The backdrop features in many of Fischer's studies of this period.

In *Variations*, an evocative solo choreographed by Fokine to Chopin's opus 69, no. 1. Photographed in 1911 by Ellis & Walery, London, who specialized in theatrical photography.

bright and natural light required less exposure time than those taken in a studio and were therefore better able to capture the action of the dance (see pages 132–133).

As early as April 1911, experiments were being made to photograph Pavlova in action during performance at the Palace Theatre, where she was making long and regular appearances. One photographer even set up his camera in the wings. Pavlova, who preferred the controlled atmosphere of a studio, was appalled at the results. Two of the most successful studies of this period, and among the first to convey the elusive, ethereal impression she gave in performance, were taken by E. O. Hoppé and Saul Bransburg. Pavlova posed for both these London photographers in costume for *Le Papillon* (see pages 120–121). Hoppé, famous for velvety, soft portraits (often retouched), held sway in his South Kensington studio, where Diaghilev sent all his dancers. Bransburg, also renowned for portraits, was happy to forsake studio settings to photograph Pavlova alfresco, often framed by leaves and holding lilies. Portraits and character studies of Pavlova were also made by such well-known photographers as Baron de Meyer and Arnold Genthe. Perhaps the finest, however, are the breathtakingly beautiful works of Eugene Hutchinson of Chicago (see page 139).

In a novel way, Pavlova's aerial quality was graphically depicted by photographers in New York during the war years. *Dragonfly* lent itself ideally to experimentation. Hill Studios, for example, photographed her against a black background on a black floor. The resulting photographs (see pages 142–143), with their various attitudes of flight, were a breakthrough in their treatment of a dance subject, and Pavlova was to be seen flying in all directions across the pages of the New York dailies and on posters announcing her appearances at the Hippodrome. "Absolutely astounding," exclaimed a writer for the *New York Review*, "and leagues ahead of the doctored negatives of a decade of acrobatic studio efforts. Whether her own conception, the skill of an inspired photographer or the efficiency of the Hippodrome press department, they are the poster triumph of the age, and will scarcely be equaled." Even Bakst dared to tilt Pavlova's image: in 1916 a silhouetted photograph of her in *Orpheus* flew horizontally across a page he designed for the souvenir program of *The Big Show*. A similar technique was used in the opening sequence of the feature film *The Dumb Girl of Portici*: through a superimposed vista of billowing clouds, Pavlova seemed to be floating on air. The presence of one or more unseen supporters was indicated only by an occasional glimpse of a glove-clad hand.

A revolution in stage photography took place in London during 1923, when the photographic department of *The Times* developed a technique for taking instantaneous shots of live performances, without the assistance of supplementary lighting or the more commonly used flashpowder. On September 10, twenty exposures varying from one-tenth to one-fortieth of a second were made from the dress circle of the Royal Opera House, Covent Garden, during a performance of *The Fairy Doll* (see pages 178–179). This breakthrough was recognized by everybody—except Pavlova. Extremely irritated by this practice, she was soon to gain a reputation for having photographers removed from the theater.

The method she preferred was devised by her versatile, globe-trotting friend James Abbe. On a stage and with supplementary lighting, he would select moments from a ballet and Pavlova would recreate them especially for the camera. There she had control. Although Abbe was one of the few people allowed to photograph her in backstage situations, Pavlova obviously had the final say, and his retouching of her feet shows that he was willing to make concessions (see page 176).

Equally compliant as Abbe were two photographers in South America, Franz van Riel and Nicolas Yaravoff. Van Riel, of Buenos Aires, was even willing to be dictated to by a third party acting as a sort of artistic overseer, advising when and from what angle he should shoot. His photographs, masterpieces of line and composition, have a remarkably modern quality. Yaravoff, a Russian expatriate in Montevideo, was also a master photographer. Depth and sensitivity were his trademarks. And in the same way that the spirit shone through Pavlova of every character that she danced, so does the essence of each ballet Yaravoff photographed seem to have been captured by his camera.

Pavlova's involvement with photography proved to be a two-edged sword. Reflecting her attitude to performance, she used every theatrical device she could to establish the character of her roles for the benefit of the camera. Never has there been a dancer more cooperative with photographers and never has there been one more insistent upon getting her own way with them. She always demanded that proofs be submitted to her, and she invariably returned them with marks across those she did not like. Her favorite photographs were those in which her feet seemed to taper away to delicate points, an effect she sometimes contrived herself by skillful shading with a pencil.

Pavlova's chosen and cultivated image of herself, albeit artificial and unreal, is not to be entirely condemned. In her image, as in her art, she would stand for nothing less than perfect beauty, and beauty, to Pavlova, meant the proud projection of the end and the concealment of its means. It was the triumph of an aesthetic ideal.

In *Assyrian Dance*, with music by Saint-Saëns, choreography by Clustine, and costume by Stowitts. Photograph by Van Riel, Buenos Aires, 1917.

PART ONE

1892–1911

Debut

A tiny figure kneels among a group of children supporting a large wicker birdcage. Taken in 1892 during her first year at the St. Petersburg Imperial Theater School, this is the earliest photograph of Anna Pavlova in performance. The ballet was *The Magic Fairy Tale*,[1] created especially for the pupils by Marius Petipa.

Six years later, Pavlova made her first solo appearance on the stage of the Maryinsky Theater. The occasion was a revival of Petipa's *Daughter of the Pharaoh* on October 21, 1898.[2] With her fellow-pupils Stanislava Belinskaya[3] and Lubov Petipa[4] she played one of the three Almahs in the second act's *grand ballabile des cariatides animées.*

Tamara Karsavina was then only thirteen and still a pupil at the ballet school, but many years later she recalled that of the three Almahs it was Pavlova who made the greatest impact: "Although perhaps technically she was the weakest, her personality and the whole poetry of her movement left the greatest impression on the public."

Ballet historian and critic Valerian Svetlov also later remembered the performance. He wrote: "Her enthusiasm for dancing and her natural gift of feeling completely at ease on the stage drew attention to themselves even then. In the *pas de trois* she spun around so violently that she finished up sitting on the prompter's box with her back to the audience. But in spite of the laughter in the hall, the youthful dancer did not lose her presence of mind. Turning gracefully to face the public, she bowed with an engaging smile, as if what had happened had been intentional and not an accident."[5]

Pavlova's innate sense of stagecraft turned an awkward moment into a charming memory. She was seventeen years old and had six months to go before her graduation.

ДОЧЬ ФАРАОНА.

БОЛЬШОЙ БАЛЕТЪ

въ 3-хъ дѣйствіяхъ и 7-ми картинахъ,

съ прологомъ и эпилогомъ.

❖━━❖

Соч. Сенъ-Жоржа и М. Петипа.

Поставленъ балетмейстеромъ М. Петипа.

Музыка Цезаря Пуни.

(Возобновленъ 21 октября 1898 г.).

Роль «Аспиччіи» исп. (въ 1-й разъ) г-жа М. Кшесинская 2.

Г-жа А. Х. Іогансонъ исполнитъ роль «Рамзеи».

Новыя декораціи: 1-я и 6-я картины — г. Ламбина; 2-я, 5-я картины и апоѳеозъ — г. Аллегри; 3-я картина — г. Смирнова; 4-я картина — г. Иванова; 7-я картина — г. Перминова. Машины и фонтанъ — г. Бергера.

Новые костюмы по рисункамъ г. Пономарева: женскіе — г-жи Офицеровой, мужскіе — г. Каффи. Головные уборы: женскіе — г-жи Терменъ, мужскіе — г. Брюно. Обувь — г-жи Левштедтъ. Парики — г. Педдера. Металлическія вещи — г. Ингинена. Бутафорскія вещи — г. Каменскаго. Трико — г-жи Добровольской.

❖━◆━❖

(*above*) Program of *Daughter of the Pharaoh*, Maryinsky Theater, October 21, 1898.
(*left*) In *The Magic Fairy Tale*. Pavlova, on the left, and Lubov Petipa are supporting the birdcage. Imperial Theaters photograph, 1892.

Giselle

One of Pavlova's earliest roles as an artist of the Imperial Ballet was Zulme, one of the two attendants to the Queen of the Wilis in the second act of *Giselle*. The attention given to Pavlova's debut in this small role on September 26, 1899,[1] was not only a tribute to her but also an indication of the growing discernment of the Russian audience. Karsavina recalled that "the overexacting public of the Maryinsky Theatre was made to realise that in Pavlova they had an exquisite and frail talent that needed careful tending." Pavlova's dancing featured none of the bravura feats of the visiting Italian ballerinas so beloved by most St. Petersburg balletomanes, but the distinguished critic Alexander Pleshcheyev noted that "there were many who considered that Italian tightrope-walking had little value."[2]

Pleshcheyev appreciated the qualities of flight and weightlessness over the virtuosity of *terre à terre* dancing, while other astute observers (Levinson and Svetlov among them) realized that Pavlova's technical limitations did not diminish her artistry, and, indeed, might even be thought to enhance it. The stiffness of her arms and the slight tension in her back were real but minor defects that would eventually be ironed out. But her lack of "turnout," the weakness in her knees, and her imperfect placement were not, even early on, necessarily viewed as flaws.

André Levinson believed that Pavlova's "deviation from the rules" set a new standard. "Pavlova's line is not merely decorative and expressive to the utmost degree," he wrote, "it is symbolic." Her arabesque, although not academically correct, he considered "a living symbol of the inexpressible."[3] Valerian Svetlov, who followed Pavlova's career from its outset, thought that her true sphere was that of the abstract dance, "the dance of the elves, sylphides, Wilis, spirits of all those poetic, ephemeral creatures that people the artistic literature of all ages and nations."[4]

(*above & left*) As Zulme. Photographs by Fischer, 1899.

Esmeralda

Petipa's 1886 restaging of Perrot's ballet in four acts and five scenes, with music by Pugni and libretto by Saint-Georges, based on Victor Hugo's *Notre Dame de Paris*. On November 21, 1899, the ballet was revived for the prima ballerina Mathilde Kchessinskaya.[1] The *grand pas des corbeilles* that opened the third act was led by Fleur de Lys (Olga Preobrajenskaya) and her two friends (Pavlova and Lubov Petipa).[2]

Photograph by Fischer, 1899.

The Seasons

Allegorical ballet in one act and four scenes, with music by Glazunov and choreography by Petipa. First performed at the Hermitage Theater, St. Petersburg, on February 7, 1900. In the opening scene Winter (Alexis Bulgakhov) was attended by an entourage of Hoarfrost, Ice, Hail, and Snow. Pavlova, in a shimmering costume by Ponamaryev, danced Hoarfrost, her first created role as a member of the Imperial Ballet.

Imperial Theaters photograph, 1900.

(*above*) In "La Sérénade." (*right*) With Fokine in "La Polonaise." Photographs by Fischer, 1900.

Harlequinade

The Hermitage Theater, linked by a bridge to the tsar's winter residence, housed a tiny stage where performances were given exclusively for members of the Imperial family and its court. Because the Russian aristocracy spoke French, and often only French, ballets premiered on the Hermitage stage were given alternate French billings.[1] Two such ballets were *The Seasons (Les Saisons)* and *Harlequinade (Les Millions d'Arlequin)*.

Only three days after the first performance of *The Seasons*, *Harlequinade* was premiered at the Hermitage Theater. Choreographed by Petipa to music by Drigo, with decors by Allegri, the two-act ballet was a mixture of mime and dance based on the traditional characterizations of the *commedia dell'arte*. Kchessinskaya played Columbine, with Preobrajenskaya as Pierrette.

The ballet was divided into twelve sequences, of which Pavlova appeared in five. She danced with Michel Fokine in the third sequence, entitled "La Sérénade," and in the immediately following "Le Rendezvous des Amoureux." She appeared with him again in "La Polonaise," the sixth sequence, and in "La Réconciliation," the ninth. In the twelfth sequence she returned to join the rest of the company in the final galop.

On February 13, 1900, at the Maryinsky Theater, *Harlequinade* and *The Seasons* were presented together for the first time at a benefit performance held in honor of Kchessinskaya's tenth anniversary with the Imperial Theaters. As a senior ballerina, Kchessinskaya was entitled to a benefit performance once every two years. Both she and Preobrajenskaya had the right to choose their roles, and, if they wished, to take sole possession of them. These were known as "monopoly roles."[2]

Pavlova was never to dance the leading role of Columbine at the Maryinsky.[3] It belonged to Kchessinskaya, who later gave it to Preobrajenskaya, who in turn bequeathed her role of Pierrette to Pavlova.[4]

Bluebeard

Fairy ballet in three acts, seven scenes, and apotheosis, with a libretto by Pashkova based on Perrault's fairy tale. Music by Schenck and choreography by Petipa. First performed at the Maryinsky Theater, December 8, 1896, at a benefit performance for Marius Petipa. Kchessinskaya created the role of Venus in the last act's "astronomical ballet." Pavlova danced Venus for the first time on September 17, 1900.[1]   Photograph by Fischer, c. 1901.

The Sleeping Beauty

Fairy ballet in three acts and prologue, with a libretto by Vsevol-ojsky and Petipa based on Perrault's fairy tale. Music by Tchaikovsky and choreography by Petipa. First performed at the Maryinsky Theater, January 3, 1890. Varvara Nikitina created the role of Florine, the Enchanted Princess, in the last act's Bluebird *pas de deux*. Pavlova's first performance of this role was on December 2, 1901.[1]   Photograph by Fischer, c. 1901.

The Awakening of Flora

According to Svetlov, it was "as a sort of test"[1] that Pavlova was given her first important role. Although she had not yet attained the rank of ballerina, she made her debut in the leading role of *The Awakening of Flora,* a one-act ballet by Petipa and Ivanov, on September 10, 1900.[2] The part of Apollo was played by her former teacher, Pavel Gerdt, with Fokine as Mercury. At later performances Fokine took over Gerdt's role.

At her debut, Pavlova was, with good reason, extremely nervous: her best qualities—her distinctive lightness and aerial delicacy—were of little use to her in a role created for the *terre à terre* technique of Kchessinskaya.[3] And, indeed, her fears of limited success were realized. Commenting on a subsequent performance, the editor of the *Petersburgskaya gazeta* said bluntly that her technique was "positively poor."[4] Another writer for the same paper was more tactful: "One thing is advisable and that is, when creating new variations for Madame Pavlova, as much attention as possible should be paid to combinations of tempi that suit the quality of her talent, i.e., airiness and elevation." This writer aptly termed her a "star who shines brightly in our choreographic sky."

If Pavlova's Flora was not altogether praiseworthy, neither was it altogether without merit. Her already highly developed sense of plastique enabled her to achieve a sculptural quality eminently suited to a ballet depicting an episode from the Greek myths, albeit one danced in strictly classical style to music by Drigo and in costumes designed by Ponamaryev with only the slightest concession to Hellenism. The almost oriental languor that Pavlova lent to her poses prompted a member of the audience recently returned from the East to remark, "The odalisques and bayadères dance like this."[5]

(*above*) As Flora. Studio portrait by Fischer, 1900.   (*left*) With Fokine as Apollo. Imperial Theaters photograph, 1900. The elaborate background is not authentic; it was painted on the original print.

King Candaule

Loosely based on events in the life of Gyges, king of Lydia, the four acts and six scenes of *King Candaule* were a fantastic blend of epochs and styles studded with spectacular pageants, battle scenes, and pastorales set by Petipa to the conventional ballet music of Pugni.

The *divertissements* in the last act opened with a *pas de trois* for the goddess Diana, the shepherd Endymion, and a satyr. This so-called *pas de Diane* was a showpiece for the ballerina. Both the opening adagio and the variation with the bow, one of Diana's traditional symbols, demanded attack, precision, and impeccable technique. Pavlova's teacher, Evgenia Sokolova, made her debut as Diana at the ballet's second St. Petersburg performance in 1868, and later prepared her protégée for the role.

Pavlova danced Diana for the first time on September 24, 1900, just two weeks after her debut as Flora. Her performance that night dispelled any doubts about her technical capabilities. At last the critics were unanimous: "Pavlova distinguished herself." They spoke of her "lightness, elegance, and grace." Plaudits were heaped on subsequent performances. Pavlova "really has the rich qualities of the first-class dancer." "Pavlova! The one who has Taglioni's feet!" raved one reviewer after her first appearance in Moscow at the Bolshoi on January 25, 1904.[1] "The St. Petersburg balletomanes are already mad about her," another one remarked, and then added with typical Muscovite reserve, "This is understandable, but in Moscow she is as yet an unknown quantity. However, she has excellent prospects."

Pavlova performed Nisia, the ballerina role in *King Candaule*, only once, on October 11, 1909,[2] but Diana was to remain among her favorites. The *pas de Diane* was included in her repertoire even after she left Russia. Titled *Les Amours de Diane* and costumed by Bakst, it was introduced at the Palace Theatre, London, on May 16, 1910.

(*above & left*) As Diana. Photograph above, c. 1907; photograph at left by Fischer, 1900.

Camargo

On January 28, 1901, *Camargo*[1] was revived by Ivanov
at the Maryinsky Theater, at a benefit performance for
Pierina Legnani, who danced the title role. Pavlova
appeared with Fokine and Georgi Kiaksht in the second
scene in a *pas de trois* to interpolated music by Baron
Wrangel, and as Snow in "The Seasons," a sequence in
the fourth scene. In her costume for Snow she posed
in Fischer's studios for this series of photographs,
which were issued as a postcard set in 1901.

With Fokine in *Camargo*, scene 2. Photograph by Fischer, 1901.

With Fokine in *Camargo*, scene 2. Photograph by Fischer, 1901.

The Magic Flute

A story of young love triumphant, *The Magic Flute* is full of comic situations for the heroine Lise and her boyfriend Luke. The young lovers are aided in their escapades by the god Oberon, who, disguised as a hermit, gives Luke a magic flute that enables him to overcome the resistance of Lise's greedy mother and to foil the wealthy old count who plans to make Lise his bride. With Nicolas Legat as Luke, Pavlova danced the part of Lise for the first time on December 19, 1901.[1]

The Magic Flute was a curtain raiser. It had been created for the pupils of the ballet school and first performed in the school theater on March 10, 1893, with Pavlova's classmate Belinskaya as Lise and Fokine as Luke. Drigo's music for it was lightweight; Ivanov's choreography was frankly uninspired.[2]

What the ballet did require was a natural aptitude for comedy, and this, with her mobile face and elfin smile, Pavlova possessed in full. The comic side of her personality is an important one that has often been overlooked. (At school she had been renowned for her incessant and brilliant mimicry of her teachers.[3])

Pavlova's dancing was impressive in spite of the ballet's negligible technical demands. As one critic put it, "The technical side of the ballet does not present any particular difficulties." And yet, "The young dancer, who has a very good *ballon* and a very charming, soft way of dancing, is as suitable for the role of Lise as is possible."[4]

(*above*) As Lise. Studio portrait by Fischer, 1901. The window was one of Fischer's standard props.
(*left*) Lise with her mother and father (J. Cecchetti and S. Gillert). Photograph by Fischer, 1901.

43

The Magic Flute

Because of its French provincial setting and its cast of
characters (particularly the heroine, Lise), *The Magic Flute*
has often been confused with the far better known *La Fille
Mal Gardée*. In fact, the *Annual of the Imperial Theaters*
for the 1901–02 season captioned several photographs
from this series by Fischer as *La Fille Mal Gardée*.
Kchessinskaya, who until 1906 held a monopoly on
the role of Lise in the latter ballet,[1] must have been
none too pleased to see this error in print.

Javotte

Javotte was premiered at the Hermitage Theater on February 12, 1902, and five days later was given its first performance at the Maryinsky. Choreographed by Gerdt to music by Saint-Saëns, with decors by Allegri, the three-act ballet was a tale of village life in provincial France. Javotte was danced by Preobrajenskaya and Gerdt was her adventurous lover, Jean. Pavlova and Fokine appeared together in a *pas d'ensemble*.

Pavlova was featured in almost every new ballet production at the Maryinsky, often in very small parts and usually partnered by Fokine. From the outset of her career she had a flair for aligning herself with the right people, not least of whom was Fokine, whose views were diametrically opposed to those of Petipa, Pavlova's intimate friend. She later justified this by maintaining that the emergence of Fokine "was made possible by Marius Petipa, who raised the ballet to such splendid heights."[1] However, in their many *pas de deux* of the early years Fokine was well aware that Pavlova was indifferent to his inner artistic turmoil.

"It became plain to me," he later wrote, "that much was unnecessary and meant nothing. After rehearsing we would sit down to rest, I would express my ideas. . . . I could see that my doubts made very little impression on her and after several of my speeches that what we were doing was not art she would reply that the audience likes it. . . . Our argument usually terminated by her telling me, 'Come on Micha, let's try it once again,' and so we rehearsed."[2]

In time, however, Pavlova became committed to Fokine's reforms, both on and off the stage. In the dancers' strike of 1905, known as the "War of the Roses," Pavlova, Fokine, and Karsavina led the progressive, or "Red Rose," faction. The following year saw the true beginning of Pavlova's artistic collaboration with Fokine, and she was to become the finest interpreter of his first creations: *The Vine* (1906),[3] *Chopiniana* (1907), *Eunice* (1907),[4] *Le Pavillon d'Armide* (1907), and *Egyptian Nights* (1908). *The Swan* (1907), a short but perfect blend of work between choreographer and dancer, marked the climax of their association.

(*above*) Studio portrait by Fischer, 1902.
(*left*) With Fokine in the *pas d'ensemble*. Photograph by Fischer, 1902.

(*above & right*) In the Olé, Act 4. Imperial Theaters photographs, undated.

Carmen

The Maryinsky Theater housed an opera company that was as important as its ballet company. The operas often included elaborate ballet sequences,[1] whether by design of the original composer or by wish of the Maryinsky management. If no ballet music existed in the original scores, appropriate dance pieces were interpolated from other sources. In either case, the opera ballets were usually choreographed by Petipa and performed by prominent members of the ballet troupe.

The dancers' contracts stipulated the number of times they were to appear during a forthcoming season. Until 1908, participation in an opera counted as one full performance. On October 16 of that year, however, the *Petersburgskaya gazeta* reported that, "according to the terms of agreement with the management, the ballerinas should dance during one season as follows: Preobrajenskaya, thirty times, Pavlova and Trefilova, forty times. Formerly performances in operas have been considered to be the same as those in ballets. Now the management considers participation in two operas to be equivalent to one performance."[2]

Opera ballets sometimes gave the younger dancers more scope to extend their range than did the regular ballet repertoire. The brilliant dance sequences interpolated in the last act of Bizet's *Carmen*[3] gave the young Pavlova a chance to demonstrate her flair for Spanish dancing. She was celebrated for her Olé, performed to Bizet's music for *L'Arlésienne*. Her looks, her speed, and her temperament made her an ideal performer of this rousing *divertissement*.

A dance from *Carmen* was included in Pavlova's repertoire at London's Palace Theatre in 1910, and a suite of dances from the opera was performed in 1915–16 during her American tour with the Boston Grand Opera Company.

The Demon

On February 23, 1902, a new production by Schkafer
of Rubinstein's opera *The Demon* was presented at
the Maryinsky Theater at a special benefit for the chorus.
In the second act Pavlova appeared in the lezghinka,
in an elaborate costume designed by Konstantin Korovin.[1]
This series of studies, by Fischer, was issued shortly afterward.

Raymonda

Ballet in three acts, four scenes, and apotheosis, with a libretto by Pashkova and Petipa. Music by Glazunov and choreography by Petipa. First performed at the Maryinsky Theater, January 7, 1898, with Legnani in the title role. The small role of Henrietta, Raymonda's friend, was performed by Pavlova in 1901.[1]

Photograph by Fischer, 1902.

La Bayadère

Ballet in four acts, seven scenes, and apotheosis,[1] with a libretto by Khudekov. Music by Minkus and choreography by Petipa. First performed at the Maryinsky Theater, January 23, 1877, with Vazem in the title role. On December 3, 1900, Pavlova danced the third variation in the Kingdom of the Shades scene.[2]

Imperial Theaters photograph, 1901.

(*above & right*) As Nikiya, in Act 2. Photographs by Fischer, 1902.

La Bayadère

La Bayadère is one of Petipa's greatest creations. This dark and complex drama involves an oriental temple dancer, Nikiya, who falls in love with and is betrayed by a handsome warrior, Solor. Nikiya, which Pavlova danced for the first time on April 28, 1902, was so far the greatest challenge she had faced.[1] Although Petipa's choreography for Nikiya did not emphasize virtuosity, it did demand great powers of expression in both dancing and acting.

Through movement and demeanor Pavlova was able not only to express Nikiya's spirit but also to suggest her oriental heritage. "In her sharp, finely molded profile, in her narrow brow decorated with a priestly headband, in her fixed gaze, one can sense the lofty, cruel austerity of an icon image."[2] And Pavlova had never been to the East.

A unique aspect of Pavlova's talent emerged at the end of the second act, when Nikiya is bitten by a snake hidden in a basket of flowers. At this point Pavlova deliberately distorted the rhythm of the dance so that her movements were no longer related to the music. This was so unusual and unexpected that it shocked the senses—confusing the eye and ear. It emphasized the isolation of the dying girl from all of those surrounding her, from the setting, and from the music. (Only by having overlooked her intuitive realization of such interpretive devices can certain critics have considered Pavlova unmusical.[3] In fact, she was instinctively otherwise.) But like every other aspect of her talent, this technique was used not as an end in itself but as another expression of character and theme.[4]

Pavlova's formidable rendering of Nikiya surpassed even Petipa's vision of the role. Characterization was sustained even into the dream sequence of the third act. Full of emotional symbolism, the dance of the departed bayadère prompted Levinson to say, "Her spectral figure emitted an icy chill. . . . She was a transparent resemblance almost deprived of flesh."[5] One would never see a dichotomy between mime and dance in any performance of Pavlova's. Throughout the ballet she danced and acted the role of Nikiya with seamless unity. Levinson recognized the artistic importance of this phenomenon: "The unrealizable in drama has become possible in the forms of the classical dance. This is the profound symbolism of ballet, realized by Pavlova."[6]

La Bayadère

In the first scene of Act 2 of *La Bayadère*,[1] Nikiya is in despair. Having discovered that Solor is betrothed to Gamzatti, daughter of the rajah, she attempts to murder her rival. These posed photographs, taken by Fischer in 1902, depict moments from this dramatic scene.

The Fairy Doll

Two young brothers who had recently risen to prominence in the St. Petersburg ballet troupe were Nicolas and Sergei Legat. Exhibiting a flair for both production and choreography, they were invited to stage a performance at the Hermitage Theater. The ballet chosen was an old Viennese one, *The Fairy Doll.*[1] An entirely new production of a little-known work, this tale of a toyshop that comes to life at night had a splendidly successful premiere at the Hermitage Theater on February 7, 1903.

The design was Léon Bakst's second for a ballet.[2] Inspired by a childhood remembrance, his toyshop on a public arcade recalled the colorful St. Petersburg Gostinny Dvor, where a fashionable row of shops with wide windows overlooked the city's main thoroughfare. The ballet was in one act and two scenes, with music by Bayer, Rubinstein, and Drigo.[3]

Pavlova's role was the Spanish Doll, who made her entrance to a furious clicking of castanets and danced to heavily syncopated rhythms and rapid tempi. Her costume by Bakst was an exquisite confection of pink and silver, with white gloves and a silver filet for her hair.

The tsar was so impressed by this production that he commanded it be included in the performance at the Maryinsky on February 16, the evening when he planned to bring his children to the ballet for the first time. The program consisted of *The Magic Flute,* in which Pavlova played the leading role of Lise; *The Fairy Doll,* in which she repeated her success as the Spanish Doll; and the *grand pas classique* from *Paquita,* in which she danced a variation. Of Pavlova's Spanish Doll Nicolas Legat wrote, "For temperament and inspirational interpretation she was unequalled."[4]

(*above & left*) As the Spanish Doll. Photographs by Fischer, 1903.

Coppélia

Petipa's restaging of Saint-Léon's three-act ballet with music by Delibes and libretto by Nuitter and Saint-Léon. This version first performed at the Bolshoi Theater, St. Petersburg, November 25, 1884. The role of one of Swanilda's friends was danced by Pavlova in her fourth season at the Maryinsky.[1]   Photograph, c. 1902.

The Magic Mirror

Fantastic ballet in four acts and seven scenes, with a libretto by Vsevolojsky and Petipa based on stories by Pushkin and the brothers Grimm. Music by Koreshchenko and choreography by Petipa. First performed at the Maryinsky Theater, February 9, 1903, when Pavlova appeared in the *pas de trois suisse*. [1]   Photograph, 1903.

Giselle

Thanks to Pavlova, *Giselle* regained its lost popularity with the St. Petersburg public.[1] Fokine, for all his dislike of this ballet, nevertheless considered Pavlova to be supreme in it. "She creates on the stage, and her talent is in harmony even with that which is inartistic."[2] To *Giselle* she brought the same vitality and imagination she had displayed in *La Bayadère* the year before. Beyond technical accomplishment, Pavlova had a special faculty for an almost improvisational creativity, which reached its pinnacle in *Giselle*. Svetlov wrote that "her powerful dramatic talent in the scene of madness and death makes you live through a moment of tragedy, and her ethereal, transparent, quivering dances in the forest among the Wilis will allow you to experience the rare instance of true artistic emotion of the highest order."[3]

On the night of April 30, 1903, Pavlova danced Giselle for the first time, with Nicolas Legat as Albrecht. At the same performance Karsavina made her debut in the peasant *pas de deux,* partnered by Fokine. Many years later Karsavina remembered that Pavlova "gave her interpretation a pathos which could not have been surpassed. The innocent gaiety of Giselle– Pavlova had the poignancy of things frail and ephemeral. The doom lying in wait for Giselle seemed all the more imminent for her unawareness. That pathos and the quality of incorporeal grace were essential features of Pavlova's genius."[4] The key to Pavlova's interpretation was its credibility. Indeed, it was to this role that she seemed to relate more personally than she did to any of her others. Before every performance of it she was always nervous in the extreme.

Perfection was achieved—but not all at once. After her much-awaited debut Svetlov observed that "somehow the touching and elegiac image of a Giselle betrayed and tragically lost . . . did not emerge,"[5] but by her next two performances in the autumn he thought that she had "mastered the role to perfection."[6] Pavlova, however, was still not satisfied. An entry made in Petipa's diary two days after her third performance records that Pavlova consulted the maestro and asked him to rehearse her privately in the mad scene.[7] Of her next performance it was reported that "Pavlova danced the dramatic mad scene artistically and in a touching manner, without exaggeration or cheap effects."[8] Giselle was a role to which Pavlova continually molded her growing talent.

(*above & left*) As Giselle, in Act 1, at the time of her debut, 1903. In previous publications the photograph on the left has been erroneously identified as Swanilda in *Coppélia*. Note the familiar backdrop in Fischer's study of the mad scene.

In *Giselle*, Act 2. Photograph by Fischer, 1903.

In *Giselle*, Act 2. Photograph by Fischer, 1903.

The Naiad and the Fisherman

This romantic tale, in three acts and five scenes, of a water sprite's infatuation with a fisherman, was on the whole unpopular. Petipa's staging of Jules Perrot's *Ondine*[1] suffered from Pugni's music, which Svetlov condemned for "unbearable banality and primitive orchestration." It produced, he said, an effect of "soporific boredom."[2]

Pavlova did, however, add a certain sparkle to the production. In the role of the Naiad, the originality she had already so superbly demonstrated in *La Bayadère* and *Giselle* revealed itself in another, lighter aspect. Svetlov called her approach to the role "intelligent" and described a moment when her supple, flowing movements in the arms of the fisherman expressed a wish to "tear herself from his grasp back into her native element."[3] Pavlova had imbued a conventional "fish dive" with dramatic meaning.

"Pavlova danced with confidence and enthusiasm," wrote Svetlov the day after her debut, "but it must be noted that her first big variation, with a long series of *brisés, pas de bourrées,* low jumps on point, and other dance 'fioritura,' is not suitable for her type of aerial talent. This is the eternal terror of all artists who try their strength in roles that do not suit them. She made up for this, however, in the 'Naiad' scene by the brilliance and élan of her variation. A consecutive number of *entrechat six,* alternating with the rarely performed double *ronds de jambe en l'air,* were danced lightly and precisely, keeping the contours of the whole body in perfect harmony."[4]

Pavlova's rapid and precise footwork throughout the ballet showed that her period of study with Caterina Beretta in Milan[5] had resulted in a considerably improved technique. In an interpolated *pas de deux*[6] she also excelled in the slow, sustained movements of the adagio. But it was her first appearance *en travesti* that was the high point of the evening. In the opening scene of the third act she appeared disguised as a fisherman. "The fisherman's attire suited her marvellously," wrote one critic, "and I would say, if this does not seem offensive, that Pavlova is an even more enchanting 'fisherman' than a 'naiad.'"[7]

Pavlova made her debut in *The Naiad and the Fisherman* on December 7, 1903, with Sergei Legat as Matteo. In retrospect, it can be seen that the role allowed her a necessary breathing space between *Giselle* and other important roles that were to follow.

(*above*) As the Naiad, at the time of her debut, 1903.   (*left*) In a "fish dive," supported by Georgi Kiaksht as Matteo, 1905.   Imperial Theaters photographs.

Paquita

Petipa's 1881 restaging of Mazilier's ballet, with libretto by Foucher and music by Deldevez, with additional music by Minkus for the *grand pas classique* and children's mazurka (Act 3) and the *pas de trois* (Act 1). The latter, which Petipa himself called his "golden *pas de trois*," was generally acknowledged to be one of his masterpieces. Pavlova received an ovation when she first appeared in it on November 21, 1901. Photograph by Fischer, 1903.

Le Corsaire

Petipa's 1863 restaging[1] of Mazilier's ballet, with music by Adam and Pugni and libretto by Saint-Georges and Mazilier, inspired by Lord Byron's poem *The Corsair*. The story of the Greek girl Medora and her adventures with a band of pirates led by the handsome Conrad. On October 9, 1902, Pavlova danced the small part of the slave Gulnare, taking over the role impromptu from the injured Trefilova.[2]   Photograph by Fischer, 1902.

Paquita

On May 2, 1904, Pavlova made her debut in the title role of *Paquita,* with Fokine as Lucien. In the *grand pas classique,* the "harp variation," which Drigo had composed especially for Pavlova, was unfortunately flawed by a few imperfect pirouettes. Svetlov, however, thought that it had the "gentle, gracious coloring of a tender, delicate drawing."[1] Another critic reported that in her second variation she "flew headlong around the stage to thunderous applause."[2] Both dances were encored.[3]

With its bolero-style Spanish dance, the dramatic mime scene of the second act was one of Pavlova's most triumphant moments. Here there was a blossoming of two of the most brilliant traits for which she had already been acclaimed. She made the transition from mime to dance every bit as smoothly and with as much continuity of character as she had in *La Bayadère.* In the dance itself, she threw off twice the grace and fire she had shown in some of her earlier Spanish roles. "He who has seen this Spanish dance in Pavlova's performance will never forget it. . . . It is how gypsies dance, full of fire and passion, in the mountains of distant Granada."[4]

At the end of the evening the balletomanes presented her with a diamond brooch. A review of the performance by Pleshcheyev appeared next morning in the *Petersburgskaya gazeta,* with a word of warning added to his praise: "The laurels and gifts should not, however, prevent Pavlova from working and working." After her second performance of *Paquita,* he observed that they had not. "The artist's technique is progressing steadily. . . . Although Paquita–Kchessinskaya is still fresh in our memories, we can watch Pavlova with rare enjoyment. One cannot say this of other Spanish girls at the Maryinsky."[5]

Throughout her career Pavlova consistently developed her interpretation of Paquita. After a performance on September 28, 1905, a critic in *Slovo* referred specifically to the *grand pas* variation: "Paradise rolled over Pavlova. . . . The sign of artistic talent vibrates in Pavlova to the extent that it positively infects the spectators. . . . It was possible to see two performances—one on the stage and the other in the auditorium."

(*above & left*) As Paquita, in the *grand pas classique*, Act 3. Photographs by Fischer, 1904.

(*above*) As Medora, in "Le Jardin Animé," Act 3. Studio portrait by Fischer, 1904.
(*right*) In the *scène dansante*, Act 2. Photograph, 1905.

Le Corsaire

At her debut as Medora, Svetlov considered that Pavlova rather overplayed the second act's "risqué" scene of seduction in the pirates' lair.[1] Attributing this single flaw in the performance to first-night nerves and certain "crudities" in the libretto, he was nevertheless favorably impressed: "I think that Byron must have dreamed of just such a Greek girl when he created his poem, because only this sort of image could inspire that sort of poet."[2]

"The qualities of a top-ranking soloist were felt decisively yesterday in all her dances, beginning with the broad flights of the entrée . . . and in the *pas d'action,* which was performed with playful coquetterie and true artistic taste. She was matchless in the *pas de deux* . . . and performed a brilliant series of *fouettés en diagonale*—so much more attractive than the commonplace 'mechanical' *fouettés.* . . . Her image of Medora was chaste and moving, but for all that poetically beautiful."[3]

Although not over-fond of the ballet itself, Pleshcheyev did admire Pavlova's performance. "It is difficult to say what was the most successful, the seduction scene, the drama with the pirates, the variation in the third act, or the character dance of the *Petit Corsaire.*"[4] He compared her to Lubov Roslavleva,[5] the Moscow ballerina and definitive Medora—"I think I cannot say anything more flattering to Pavlova than that she resembled Roslavleva, although of course she was not completely equal to her"—and went on to say that Medora was "far from being the principal role in Pavlova's repertoire."[6]

Pavlova's romantic approach to the role was particularly admired. When in the *grand pas d'action* ("Le Jardin Animé," to music by Delibes)[7] she bourréed among garlands of flowers, Pleshcheyev said that she reminded him of lithographs of Grisi and Taglioni. In her variation in the same scene she performed an exquisitely delineated series of *cabrioles,* "amazing for their breadth, suppleness, and ethereal quality."[8] Her *ballon* throughout the ballet was so extraordinary that one critic was completely carried away: "Pavlova danced. No, she did not dance, she fluttered. No, she did not flutter, she soared. . . . If she put on a hat with two bird feathers, you would not hold her on the ground with ropes."[9]

When Pavlova made her debut as Medora on December 5, 1904, with Gerdt as Conrad, she was already an established favorite with the St. Petersburg public. Pleshcheyev noted the "special Pavlova applause," which, he said, resounded at intervals "like shots from a gun."

Don Quixote

On December 4, 1905, Pavlova made her debut as Kitri
in Alexander Gorsky's restaging[1] of Petipa's ballet to music by
Minkus with decors and costumes by Golovin and Korovin.
Pavlova gave Kitri the full-blooded characterization
that became a model for every subsequent interpreter
at the Maryinsky. These studies by Fischer were issued
as a postcard set and show Pavlova in moments
from the tavern scene in Act 2.

(*above & right*) As Bint-Anta, in Gorsky's version of the ballet. Photographs taken in Fischer's Moscow studio, 1906. The photograph at right shows Pavlova's first entrance.

Daughter of the Pharaoh

Pavlova's association with Gorsky was renewed when, on January 15, 1906, she appeared at the Bolshoi Theater in his controversial production of Petipa's *Daughter of the Pharaoh.*[1] "Her first entrance was met with scanty applause, from the confirmed ballet enthusiasts, but soon they were joined by the rest of the audience. . . . Pavlova drove the Muscovites into transports with her flights, her outstanding elevation, and the general brio of her performance."[2]

The rambling plot of the original Petipa version had been loosely based on a story by Théophile Gautier: an English explorer fantasizes a series of adventures with Aspicia, daughter of Ramses II. Petipa's strictly classical choreography was danced to some most un-Egyptian music composed by Pugni. Roller's monumental decors and the occasional motif on some of the costumes were in fact the only concessions made to an Egyptian style.

If Petipa's production, which dated from 1862, was illogical, Gorsky's 1905 version was ludicrous—and Petipa loathed it. Attempting to introduce an element of authenticity, Gorsky had the dancers move in profile in order to create the impression of two-dimensional Egyptian frescoes. But this posture was not used consistently in the dance passages. The erratic style of dance and mime was matched by Korovin's erratic costuming: his effectively Egyptian creations alternated with conventional nineteenth-century ballet uniforms.

If she noticed them at all, the eclectic Pavlova ignored these inconsistencies. Her own imaginativeness lent itself quite readily to the certain amount of improvisation for which Gorsky's choreography allowed, and she learned the role of the Egyptian princess, whom Gorsky had renamed Bint-Anta, in only two rehearsals.

Just two weeks later, on January 29, Pavlova played Aspicia in Petipa's production at the Maryinsky Theater. In the prologue, Aspicia made her entrance bedecked with jewels. Kchessinskaya, a court favorite, always wore her own jewelry; Pavlova's was artificial. In the third act, Kchessinskaya came up from the depths of the Nile bone-dry. When Pavlova emerged from the water, the folds of her long chemise seemed to cling to her body.

On the night of her St. Petersburg debut in *Daughter of the Pharaoh,* playing to a packed house, Pavlova broke Kchessinskaya's monopoly on the role of Aspicia. Teliakovsky recorded in his diary that "it was like a celebration of the end of slavery."

Daughter of the Pharaoh

The *grand pas de crotales* in the last act of Gorsky's
Daughter of the Pharaoh showed to perfection the filigree
delicacy of Pavlova's line, the proud arch of her instep,
and the strength of her supple back. The virile splendor
and superb technique of Mikhail Mordkin provided an
ideal complement. These photographs were taken in
1906 in Fischer's Moscow studios.

Raymonda

Pavlova made her debut in the Panaderos, the fiery Spanish dance in the second act of *Raymonda,* on October 29, 1906. One of her most successful dances, invariably encored, it was included in the repertoire of her German tour in 1908, when she posed for this portrait in her magnificient blue and silver costume at Schneider's studios in Berlin. Photographs of this role have been erroneously identified as Kitri in *Don Quixote.*

Don Quixote

Even more sensational was Pavlova's unexpected appearance as
both Mercedes and the Street Dancer on September 2, 1907, in
the opening performance of the season. Pavlova, by now one of
the top four ballerinas at the Maryinsky, was unique in her will-
ingness to dance secondary roles. This study of her as Mercedes
in her Korovin-designed costume was taken by Fischer in 1907.
In both photographs she is wearing her own diamond necklace.

Le Pavillon d'Armide

From its very inception, *Le Pavillon d'Armide* was beset with problems. The composer Tcherepnin and the designer-librettist Benois had for more than six years been attempting to have it staged at the Maryinsky. On April 15, 1907, Fokine mounted one scene from it for the ballet school's graduation performance. This scene, entitled *The Animated Gobelin,* was so successful that it was included in the repertoire of the small touring group, headed by Pavlova and Fokine, that opened a season in Moscow a few weeks later. It was there, on May 25, that Pavlova played Armida for the first time. In the autumn of the same year, Kchessinskaya, who was to have played Armida in the three-scene version at the Maryinsky, withdrew from the role, and Pavlova lost no time in offering to replace her.

In spite of following a rather dull performance of *Swan Lake,* and being relegated to the end of the evening, the premiere on November 25 was an immediate success. Benois remembers that Pavlova kissed him and that Diaghilev rushed up to him, exclaiming, "We must take this abroad!"[1]

Fokine's ballet was an integrated mosaic of music and movement, and could not be dominated by the ballerina. For the first time in her career, Pavlova was overshadowed. If anyone did shine out, it was not her, but the eighteen-year-old Vaslav Nijinsky. The part of Armida's slave had been written into the ballet especially for him. Not surprisingly, Pavlova herself did not care for the work, probably for the same reason that Kchessinskaya withdrew: as Svetlov put it, "The role of Armida is static and bereft of any psychological conflict."[2]

Despite the limitations of the role, Pavlova brought a great range of subtle emotions to Armida. The moment when she emerged from the tapestry "with her arms outstretched and her blazing eyes staring fixedly into a world unseen,"[3] was particularly memorable. From a dancing point of view, the high point of her performance was the *pas de deux* with Nijinsky. Their partnership was to last fewer than six years.[4] That it was so brief is regrettable; that it was so perfect is one of the glories of ballet history.

(*above & left*) As Armida. Photographs by Fischer, 1907.

Le Pavillon d'Armide

In 1907 Pavlova and Nijinsky posed in Fischer's studios for a series of studies of *Le Pavillon d'Armide*. This was probably the only time they faced a camera together. For this reason alone these photographs are among the most historic in the annals of ballet photography.

Chopiniana

In 1907 Fokine was invited to create an evening of ballet for a charity performance at the Maryinsky on February 10. One of the ballets presented on this occasion was based on a suite of four Chopin pieces—a polonaise, a nocturne, a mazurka, and a tarantella—orchestrated by Glazunov in 1892. To these Fokine added Chopin's Waltz in C Sharp Minor (op. 64, no. 2), which he had asked Glazunov to orchestrate.

Fokine's "first *Chopiniana*" was divided into five tableaux: the polonaise was set in a stately ballroom; the nocturne, in a monastery; the mazurka, in a Polish wedding scene; the waltz was danced by Pavlova and Mikhail Obukhov as a *pas de deux* in the style of Taglioni;[1] and the tarantella was performed before a vista dominated by Mount Vesuvius.[2]

Pavlova's performance of the waltz inspired much choreographic interest in Chopin's music. In the autumn of the same year Fokine created *Pas des Papillons* to the "Minute Waltz," which he danced with Pavlova at a benefit for Marie Petipa.[3] On the same evening Nijinsky appeared with Kchessinskaya in a *pas de deux* choreographed by Kulichevskaya to a Chopin nocturne. On March 8, 1908, Fokine's "second *Chopiniana*" was premiered at the Maryinsky, under the title *Ballet to the Music of Chopin.* (On April 6, 1908, it was mounted for the graduating pupils of the ballet school as *Grand Pas to the Music of Chopin.*)

The clashing styles and ethnic settings of the "first *Chopiniana*" had been left behind, but the romantic atmosphere of the original waltz remained, and prevailed throughout the ballet. As well as the *pas de deux* of the first version, there were four solo variations and two ensembles, orchestrated by Maurice Keller. The ballet was preceded by Chopin's Polonaise in A Major (op. 40, no. 1), orchestrated by Glazunov. Pavlova appeared in the opening Nocturne in A Flat Major (op. 32, no. 2), the Mazurka in D Major (op. 33, no. 2), the closing Waltz in E Flat Major (op. 18), and the *pas de deux,* on this occasion partnered by Nijinsky.

In her solo mazurka, Pavlova "barely touched the floor with her toes. She flew across the stage in a zig-zag, leaving a melodious trace behind her."[4] "If one measured this flight in terms of inches, it actually would not be particularly high. . . . Pavlova had mastered the difference between jumping and soaring, which is something that cannot be taught."[5]

(*above & left*) In her favorite costume, of white muslin trimmed with garlands of pink silk rosebuds. This was probably the first Bakst costume to be seen in the West. Photographs by Schneider, Berlin, 1908.

(*above*) The entrance of the Swan. Photograph unidentified but probably taken in Berlin, 1908.   (*right*) The death of the Swan. Photograph by Hänse Herrmann, Berlin, 1908.

The Swan

The Maryinsky Theater. December 22, 1907.[1] A wave of amazement flooded over the house as a slim figure in a white tutu drifted across the darkened stage with her back to the audience.

"Pavlova as the Swan rises on tiptoe, crossing her lowered arms on her feathered tunic, and dreamily describes slow circles. Impelled by the rhythmic swaying of her arms, she rushes into the depths of the stage to meet the imaginary horizon on the backcloth. Prepared for flight, she comes to a halt, as though on the edge of an airy precipice, in a tense, beautiful *attitude*. Suddenly her figure is inclined in pain, and her arms clasped to her body bend excruciatingly in abrupt movements of agony and struggle. Her steps become quick and irregular in her alarm. On legs quivering like strings, she moves backward toward the footlights. Darting one leg forward in a magnificently curved ascent, she lands on one knee, and with her dying motion, protracted and indescribably moving, she finally comes to rest."[2]

The classical elements of the choreography—a starkly simple sequence of *pas de bourrées* broken only by an occasional *attitude*—served to heighten the newfound freedom immediately evident in the singularly unclassical, expressive use of the arms.

Innovatory, too, was the choice of music. The episode from Saint-Saëns' *Carnaval des Animaux* lacked any of the obvious trademarks of conventional ballet music. Furthermore, it was used not in any strict rhythmical sense but to create an ambiance for the dance. A parallel may be drawn here to melodeclamation, a form of dramatic recitation to musical accompaniment popular in St. Petersburg at the time.[3] As in melodeclamation, in Fokine's dance monologue it was more in a spiritual than a technical sense that the music was relevant.

Pavlova's appearance on the Maryinsky stage in the traditional white costume associated with *Swan Lake*[4] was ironical indeed. Odette, the Swan Queen, was never included in her Russian repertoire.[5] Yet because of Pavlova's Swan all subsequent interpreters of Odette looked at the role with new eyes. Fokine's solo, created almost by chance in a matter of minutes, a synthesis of the traditional and the modern, proved that a controlled expressiveness could work within, and be enhanced by, a classical frame. If for no other reason, *The Swan* is a landmark in ballet history. As Krasovskaya has said, "The choreographer and dancer created in this dance a monument to each other that became a monument to an epoch."[6]

The Swan

Of the hundreds of photographs of Pavlova in *The Swan* among the finest are those by Hänse Herrmann, taken in Berlin in 1908, three of which are reproduced here. The photograph on the right is one of a series taken in London by Saul Bransburg in 1912.

Swan Lake

In the spring of 1908 Pavlova and Adolph Bolm led a company of twenty dancers from the Maryinsky Ballet on a tour of Scandinavia and Germany.[1] Act 1, scene 2, of *Swan Lake* was included in their repertoire, and at last Pavlova had the opportunity to dance Odette.

In Berlin, the praise evoked by the dancing in *Der Schwanenteich (Swan Pond),* was of a high, if somewhat unusual, order. Pavlova's performance was reviewed rather as if she were a visiting soprano. "I would call her a coloratura dancer," declared one critic, "inasmuch as her feet have the same kind of mobility, elasticity, and fluidity . . . as the ear perceives from a coloratura singer. The toe dancing of Pavlova is of immense strength, and the speed at which she spins induces dizziness."[2]

Curtly dismissed, however, was Pavlova's beautiful costume by Bakst. "As far as costumes are concerned, the Russian ballet is still behind us. They still favor the short little white skirts. . . . Here we have adopted long, flowing robes."[3]

During the following year, a tour of Berlin, Leipzig, Prague, and Vienna included a three-act version of *Swan Lake,* in which Pavlova was partnered by Nicolas Legat as Siegfried. Almost two hours of "toe dancing" to Tchaikovsky's music proved too much for the critics to bear. One of them even had difficulty in following the plot, although he did realize that "something was amiss."[4] The music was variously described as "not very good, but decent," "boring," and "old-fashioned."

One Berlin critic, after asserting that Tchaikovsky must be a disappointment to anyone who wanted to hear "intellectual music," went on to make an even more extraordinary statement: "Pavlova is not only a dancer of phenomenal skill, but a very prominent personality of a somewhat Mongolian type."[5]

(*above*) As Odette, with Legat as Siegfried. Photograph by Schneider, Berlin, 1909.
(*left*) In arabesque. Photograph by Zander & Labisch, Berlin, 1908.

La Fille Mal Gardée

One of Pavlova's favorite roles was Lise in *La Fille Mal Gardée*.[1]
The three-act ballet, with music by Hertel and choreography
by Petipa and Ivanov, was included in her first tours abroad,
when she was partnered by Bolm (1908) and Legat (1909).
These photographs were taken in the Schneider
studios in Berlin in 1908 or 1909.

Giselle

Giselle, which was included in both the 1908 and 1909 tours, came to Berlin at a most opportune time. With Isadora Duncan's appearances still fresh in their memories, the Berliners welcomed *Giselle* and Pavlova with open arms.

"Fortunately, Isadora Duncan has not been able to eliminate the art of dancing at a time when in all spheres of the arts the tendency is toward getting away from technique. The ballet ensemble of the Maryinsky Theater . . . had a sensational success of the first order, which was very well deserved. The critics can only join the audience in its rousing enthusiasm. The pirouettes of Pavlova, her excellent technique of toe dancing, the grace of her beautiful, slim body, and her unsurpassed mime enjoyed a triumph above all expectations."[1]

Although her acting and her "tiptoe coloratura" were praised, her wraithlike beauty was less admired in Vienna. "Unfortunately, she is neither beautiful nor perfectly shaped, but *thin,* like most of her Russian colleagues. This does not enhance her art."[2] Such was the verdict of one critic, who added insult to insult by comparing Pavlova unfavorably to the buxom beauties of the Viennese court opera ballet. As far as this critic was concerned, the "Tolstoyan gloom" that permeated Pavlova's Giselle was instantly dispelled by her Panaderos in the following *divertissements.* "I liked her better as a Spanish lady—at least her two black eyes were looking upward." Pavlova's eyes were "surely the key to the being of this very interesting person."

Another Viennese critic thought Pavlova's Giselle "magnificent" and praised her virtuoso pointwork and her "movements of superhuman finesse," but thought that the ballet itself "had not improved" since its last performance in Vienna. "*Giselle* will soon be seventy years old, and you can feel it."[3]

Despite the mixed reviews, the visit of the Russian ballet was highly successful. The 1909 tour ended in Vienna. There, on May 30, an extra performance[4] replaced the advertised opera, *Elektra.* Within three days Pavlova was dancing in Paris with the troupe assembled by Diaghilev for his Saison Russe.

(*above*) As Giselle, in Act 2, with Legat as Albrecht. Pavlova's costume, designed by Bakst especially for her, is remarkably similar to the costumes for the Maryinsky version and for *Chopiniana*.   (*left*) In Act 1. The white silk dress, trimmed with blue ribbon and appliquéd with tiny blue flowers, was also designed by Bakst.   Photographs by Schneider, Berlin, 1909.

Les Sylphides

Fokine's "second *Chopiniana*" had been given its new French title at Diaghilev's insistence. Described in the Paris program as a "romantic reverie in one act," the ballet had been polished to perfection. The finishing touches were provided by Alexandre Benois' romantic costumes and his set depicting a gothic ruin bathed in moonlight. Gone was the inappropriate Polonaise in A Major that had preceded the former version. In its place was the Prelude in A Major (op. 28, no. 7). New orchestrations of the Chopin piano pieces had been provided by Stravinsky, Sokolov, Liadov, and Taneyev; only the *pas de deux* was danced to the original orchestration by Glazunov.

Weeks before Pavlova's arrival in Paris her picture was to be seen all over the city. Huge publicity posters heralding Diaghilev's 1909 Saison Russe at the Théâtre du Châtelet[1] bore Serov's sketch of Pavlova in *Les Sylphides*. And it was in this ballet, on June 2, 1909, that Paris saw her dance for the first time.

The French instantly recognized the phenomenon of Pavlova. "All the essentials of the dance, nobility of gesture, beauty of line, lightness, elevation, have united in her to produce the ideal dancer."[2] "A *feu sacré* burns in her. Mere technical precision is not her goal. When she dances the result is . . . a masterpiece."[3] Recalling the impact of Pavlova and Nijinsky in *Les Sylphides,* Serge Grigoriev later wrote, "If Nijinsky was compared to Vestris, Pavlova, in the opinion of all who saw her, was a second Taglioni."[4]

"Taglioni was Pavlova's ideal," wrote Fokine. "Did Pavlova attain her ideal? Is it not possible that she surpassed it?"[5]

(*above & left*) In the Benois costume for *Les Sylphides*. Photographs by Bert, Paris, 1909. One year later, in 1910, Karsavina posed for the same photographer in—curiously enough—this same costume for the famous *Giselle* series with Nijinsky.

(*above*) As Ta-Hor.   (*right*) With Fokine as Amoun.   Photographs by Bert, Paris, 1909.

Cléopâtre

Fokine's *Egyptian Nights* had been premiered at the Maryinsky on March 8, 1908, on the same evening as his "second *Chopiniana*." Pavlova created the role of Veronica,[1] and Fokine played the young hunter Amoun, with whom she is in love. In return for his life, Cleopatra offers Amoun one night of love. Veronica begs him to resist in vain. A high priest saves the day by substituting a sleeping draught for the poison cup that Cleopatra forces Amoun to drink.

Egyptian Nights became *Cléopâtre* on the same evening and for the same Parisian audience that had seen the "second *Chopiniana*" transformed into *Les Sylphides*. For this production Veronica was renamed Ta-Hor. Neither Ida Rubinstein's sensational Cleopatra nor Fokine's brilliant rendition of Amoun could overshadow Pavlova's "magnificently tragic"[2] Ta-Hor, "supple and subtle as a Nile reed."[3]

If *Les Sylphides* was popular, *Cléopâtre* was overwhelming. Diaghilev had worked a miracle. An exotic decor by Bakst had replaced the makeshift backdrop from *Aida* that had served for the St. Petersburg performance. Arensky's score was supplemented with music by Taneyev, Rimsky-Korsakov, Glinka, Mussorgsky, and Glazunov. And here was no happy ending: Amoun downed the fatal poison while Pavlova–Ta-Hor (the sylphide of less than an hour ago) beat her breast and rent her hair.

Pavlova was an "ardent devotee"[4] of Fokine's reforms and was quite willing to sacrifice her personality to the requirements of the role. For Veronica, and later for Ta-Hor, Fokine gave Pavlova "a sample of the color to be used on the body evenly to appear like an Egyptian girl."[5] Allowing him to elongate her eyes with makeup, and sharpen the contours of her mouth, she who was by now a ballerina was prepared to go onstage in virtual disguise. She submitted "wholeheartedly and with inspiration"[6] to Fokine's demands. "At that time, to me and even to Pavlova herself, it became clear that her power, her charm, was not in this or that technical trick . . . but in her ability to create an artistic image."[7]

Le Festin

Pressed for time in which to create the closing item for his Parisian season's triple bill, Diaghilev quickly put together a thoroughly derivative *potpourri* and called it *Le Festin.* This series of dances from various operas and ballets in the repertoire of the Imperial Theaters was performed before Korovin's set for the first scene of *Russlan and Ludmilla.*

Of the nine pieces, two had been choreographed by Petipa. Karalli and Mordkin, supported by eight couples, danced the *grand pas hongrois* from the last act of *Raymonda.* Magnificently costumed by Bakst, the Bluebird *pas de deux* danced by Karsavina and Nijinsky was the glittering focal point of *Le Festin.* For reasons best known to Diaghilev, it appeared under the title *L'Oiseau de Feu.* The only new piece of choreography was a rather unsatisfactory number by Fokine for the finale, to the march from Tchaikovsky's Second Symphony.

Purely by chance, *Le Festin* was the last ballet presented during Diaghilev's 1909 Saison Russe. The *pièce de résistance* he had planned for the farewell gala at the Opéra on June 19 did not materialize. The evening was to have concluded with a performance of *Giselle,* in which Nijinsky was to have made his debut as Albrecht, partnering the ballet's supreme interpreter, Pavlova. Only the sudden illness of Nijinsky caused the last-minute cancellation of an event heralded by the Paris press as *"absolument sensationnel."* [1]

Typically, Diaghilev snatched triumph from the jaws of disaster. For the much anticipated *Giselle* he quickly substituted a truncated *Les Sylphides* and a reshuffled version of *Le Festin,* featuring Pavlova. Nijinsky was replaced by George Rosai in *L'Oiseau de Feu,* which was relegated to a reworked finale, as was *Grand Pas Hongrois,* now reduced to six couples. By refocusing *Le Festin* on Pavlova, Diaghilev at last gave her an opportunity to display her virtuosity, theretofore denied her by the Fokine-dominated repertoire of the Paris season. [2] In the featured spot normally occupied by Karsavina and Nijinsky, Pavlova and Mordkin appeared in a new item bearing the anonymous title *Pas de Deux.*

This was a *pas de deux* from Gorsky's *Daughter of the Pharaoh,* minus the entrée and coda. The opening adagio, danced to music by Bleichmann, was followed by variations for Mordkin and Pavlova to music by Tchaikovsky and Bartlett. Of Mordkin's costume there is neither photograph nor written description. Of Pavlova, however, there are two photographs by Bert in which she wears a startling Egyptian costume closely resembling several of her *Daughter of the Pharaoh* costumes—but identical to none of them. The costume would never be seen again, but the *pas de deux* itself would reappear in numerous versions and sundry disguises.

(above & left) As she appeared at the Paris Opéra in 1909. Photographs by Bert, Paris, 1909.

Russian Dance

In the summer of 1909 Pavlova and Mordkin performed
Russian Dance on two particularly notable occasions.
On June 26 they danced it at a charity gala at the
Paris Opera.[1] On July 19 they presented it in London at
a private party given by Lord and Lady Londesborough[2]
and attended by the king and queen of England.[3]
This spectacular *pas de deux,* arranged by Mordkin to
Tchaikovsky's "Danse Russe," included a variation for
Pavlova set to Alabiev's "Nightingale." She posed at the
studios of Ellis & Walery in her elaborate Bilibin-designed
sarafan of white and gold tissue for this set of photographs,
the first to be taken of her in London.

(*above & right*) As Swanilda, in the black and gold costume designed by Prince Schervachidze.
Photographs by Campbell-Gray, London, c. 1910.

Coppélia

Pavlova's first entrance upon the stage of New York's Metropolitan Opera House on February 28, 1910, was greeted by total silence. Because the management would not sanction an entire evening of ballet, the curtain did not rise on the first scene of *Coppélia*[1] until almost eleven o'clock, when a third of the "sedate Monday night gathering"[2] had already left, having had their money's worth in the form of a star-studded performance of Massenet's *Werther*.

Such indifference toward ballet was not, however, shared by everyone, and those who remained soon broke their silence. "After the first waltz which immediately follows her entrance, the audience burst into vociferous applause which was thereafter repeated at every possible opportunity."[3] "She received an ovation at the hands of the audience which Enrico Caruso or any other golden-throated tenor would have been proud to receive."[4]

The state of ballet in America at this time can be gauged from a headline that appeared in the *New York Times* on the day of Pavlova's Metropolitan debut: "Pavlova to Help Revive the Ballet, Russian Dancers from St. Petersburg Represent the Traditions of the Classic School." This was followed by the amazing revelation that in St. Petersburg "Two Nights a Week Are Given Over Exclusively to the Ballet in the Imperial Opera House."

Pavlova's physical beauty provoked much comment. The Americans compared her to Lina Cavalieri, and they loved the slimness that had been so denigrated by the Viennese. As one critic put it, "Her limbs have none of the muscular development that ordinarily accompanies this sort of dancing."[5] The critics also noted the bewitching drollness that Pavlova brought to the part of Swanilda, particularly in the scene where she impersonated the dolls.

It says much for the American critics that, while they appreciated the dazzling virtuosity of Pavlova and Mordkin, they were able to do so with discernment. "What other dancers, on the technical side, do considerately Miss Pavlova accomplishes vaporously. . . . What, with men of the ballet, would be a feat, Mr. Morkdin makes an impulse. . . . Other dancers dance with their technique. They dance by their technique with their spirits."[6]

(*above*) As she appeared at the Palace Theatre in 1910. Photograph by Foulsham & Banfield, London, 1910.   (*right*) Pavlova and Mordkin as they appeared at the Metropolitan Opera House in 1910. Photograph by Mishkin, New York, 1910.

Pas de Deux

On the evening after her success in *Coppélia,* Pavlova danced with Mordkin again at the Metropolitan Opera House, at a charity gala.[1] With such an electrifying showpiece as Bleichmann's *Pas de Deux,* they were well armed to face the competition of the established favorites who were also to appear, such as Enrico Caruso and Emmy Destinn. This was the same *pas de deux* that in 1909 had made its unexpected appearance in Paris, in *Le Festin.* Having been excluded from the Parisian version, the entrée and the coda were reinstated here.

Mordkin, who "darted on to the stage dressed as a savage"[2] in his *Daughter of the Pharaoh* costume, proceeded to perform a solo with a bow and arrow. He had choreographed this spectacle himself to the music for the Prince's variation in the last act of *The Sleeping Beauty.* (So wildly successful was this solo that it later became famous as *Bow and Arrow Dance,* and constituted a separate item in future programs.) Wearing a variant of one of her Korovin-designed costumes from *Daughter of the Pharaoh,* Pavlova "twirled on her toes. With her left toe pointed out behind her, maintaining her body posed to form a straight line with it, she leapt backward step by step on her right foot. She swooped into the air like a bird and floated down. She never dropped. At times she seemed to defy the laws of gravitation."[3]

It was in this *pas de deux* that on April 18, 1910, Pavlova and Mordkin made their debut at the Palace Theatre, London. While Mordkin still sported his metallic-looking tunic from *Daughter of the Pharaoh,* Pavlova's costume (described by *The Times* as "the traditional costume of Columbine") was a copy of an original designed by Prince Schervachidze for Kchessinskaya. The program boldly announced that *Pas de Deux* had been "arranged by Mordkin"; Gorsky's name was nowhere to be seen. While Mordkin had certainly choreographed his own variation, it is unlikely that he had had anything to do with Pavlova's, danced to the pizzicato from Delibes' *Sylvia* and revealing "an astonishing power of dancing and whirling on one toe."[4]

Pas de Deux did, however, go through an amazing number of choreographers both in future seasons at the Palace and on the provincial tours. Continually subjected to changes of costume, and with its choreographers (and composers) gaily playing a game of musical chairs, this seemingly innocuous *pas de deux* became the ballet historian's nightmare.[5]

Valse Caprice

With its backbends, its runs, and its astonishing lifts, it is difficult to believe that *Valse Caprice* was choreographed at the turn of the century. This *pas de deux* to the music of Rubinstein was arranged by Nicolas Legat, who danced it with Olga Preobrajenskaya at a benefit performance at the Maryinsky on February 4, 1901.[1] It is the prototype of the Russian *divertissement* that was to become so popular in the West during the 1950s tours of the Bolshoi Ballet. *Valse Caprice* was first seen in the West when Legat and Kchessinskaya performed it in Vienna in 1903.[2] Pavlova and Mordkin danced it at their first night at the Palace.

It was one of the finest dances they ever performed, and it was through them that this brief lyrical interlude, this "etherialized village courtship," had the power to drive the London audience wild. The contrast between the sylphlike Pavlova, "floating in a cloud of the airiest fabric which ever held together,"[3] and the majestically proportioned Mordkin could well have been glaring and even grotesque. Between the two, however, there was a special chemistry that gave spirited grace to the chase and charm to the final capture.

"To see her in his arms throwing back her head in an attitude of would-be escape brings the house to that point of murmured admiration which is very rarely heard in England."[4] "The whole dance was as delicious as a perfect lyric in its gay spontaneity and its impeccable beauty of detail."[5] "None have ever approached these two in grace of movement, artistic effect, and amazing beauty of pose. . . . Their art is beyond criticism, certainly beyond all argument."[6]

A critic of *The Graphic*, however, found reason to voice a complaint: "In a second dance the old and the new methods are patched indecorously together; the feet of Pavlova are the feet of the ballet-girl, though the garments and hands are the garments and hands of Isadora. It is to me peculiarly irritating to see this tenderly veiled sylph dotting it about as if she had lost both her legs in battle, and had to do the best she could with stilts. Here Mordkin is little more than gentleman in attendance to give her a lift when required (and what, I wonder, is meant by his silly little knickers)."[7]

(*above*) One of a series of photographs posed at London's Dover Street Studios, 1910.
(*left*) Studio portrait from the same period.

Valse Caprice

Pavlova and Mordkin posed for this series of photographs
of *Valse Caprice* in London's Dover Street Studios in
April 1910. Comprising one of the finest records of their
partnership ever made, these photographs are presented
together here for the first time as a series.

Bacchanale

"The most frantic dance that choreography has ever known," *Bacchanale*[1] was the third *pas de deux* presented on opening night at the Palace. Even the Isadora Duncan devotees were satisfied. The little Greek sandals for which, in this dance, Pavlova had discarded her ballet shoes must be partly held to account for one critic's rapturous appraisal: "And then in a third dance Isadora is all but absolute victor. It is a Bacchic rhapsody to the tune of Rubinstein [*sic*], and the two devotees leap out of hiding to the sound of pipes, dishevelled, heads tossing, with electric verve and wine-fired jubilation. Our blood burns to join in the measure. Recklessly they beckon and entice. . . . And the feet come up prancing recklessly, and the heads bend down, and the eyes and the teeth flash thirsty laughter. And then the nymph cuddles herself deliciously up to the satyr and then throws herself away from him in a glorious curve of abandonment, and we shout applause. . . ."[2]

Although a reckless spirit of abandon did in this piece reign supreme, the idea of Pavlova as a proselyte or interpreter of Isadora Duncan's ideas is erroneous and absurd. Pavlova's dancing had an underlying control that Duncan's dances never had, and their respective bacchic frenzies sprang from completely different sources. There was, however, a small dispute over how frenzied, or "bacchanalian," the dance really was. Although the reserved Cyril Beaumont considered it "extremely abandoned,"[3] the critic of *The Times* was left with the impression that the dancers "could hardly be ungraceful if they tried."[4]

But even the most imperturbable critics could not deny the frenzied nature of an incident that took place in the wings one evening during the following season. The sound that was made by Pavlova's hand as it struck Mordkin's cheek was heard in the auditorium. For several days Pavlova and Mordkin refused to dance together. On April 27 they were reunited, and the performance was the best they had ever given. "When they rush on together, nymph and faun beneath that flaming veil, is it possible that ever before was there such a glorious frenzy? . . . The splendid tumult of it all, the mad delight in power, the divine intoxication with the wonder of the world—was that ever so vivid, ever with such a thrill?"[5]

(*above*) The entrance of Pavlova and Mordkin.   (*left*) As the Bacchante.
Photographs by Mishkin, New York, 1910.

Mishkin's famous series of photographs of Pavlova and Mordkin in *Bacchanale,* taken during their first visit to New York, was featured in the prestigious London *Tatler* on April 20, 1910. The caption that ran across the illustrated center spread announced "The Greatest Dancer in the World, Another 'Catch' for the Palace Theatre."

117

The Legend of Azyiade

Oriental ballet in one act with music by Rimsky-Korsakov, Chaminade, Arensky, Glazunov, and Bourgault-Ducoudray, choreography by Mordkin, and decor by Goloff. An exotic tale of a barbaric chieftain and his captive Azyiade, who finally gains her freedom when her self-indulgent captor falls into a drunken stupor. First performed in New York on October 15, 1910. Photograph of Pavlova and Mordkin by White, New York, 1910.

Souvenir d'Espagna

Pas de trois with music by Gillet, choreography by Chiriaieff, and costumes by Diatchkoff. A lively Spanish romp in which a flirtatious lady teases her two cavaliers. Included on Pavlova's 1911–12 provincial tour of England and later performed at the Palace. In billing, Pavlova consistently preferred to spell *Espagne* with a final *a,* as given above. Photograph of Laurent Novikoff (left), Pavlova, and Peter Zajlich by Bransburg, London, 1912.

Le Papillon

This solo was the brightest, gayest, fastest, shortest, and most demanding of Pavlova's repertoire.[1] In Bakst's dazzling costume she flashed and fluttered across the stage—a green and gold blur—her tapering feet performing the tiniest *pas de bourrées* imaginable to the tinkling harp music that all the world knows today as Kitri's variation from the last act of *Don Quixote*.[2] "Butterflies have souls; Pavlova proved it, for she must have seized a butterfly's very being and encompassed it with her own. It was a direct impersonation of a butterfly, floating, sipping, quivering with the joy of life; as indifferent to everything as one of those iridescent little bubbles you see beginning its career at the bottom of the tube of a champagne glass, intoxicated with its own beauty, filled with the sunshine that grapes have absorbed, and knowing it was a microcosm of beauty."[3]

(*above*) Hoppé's favorite study of Pavlova, London, c. 1911.
(*left*) Photograph by Bransburg, London, c. 1911.

(*above*) This drawing by Frank Haviland was reproduced on a full page of the *Illustrated London News*, December 2, 1911. The costume is a variant of the one designed by Bakst for Karsavina in 1909. (*right*) Posing in the garden at her rented home in Golders Green, London, 1911.

L'Oiseau d'Or

On June 24, 1911, *The Times* observed that in *Le Papillon* "Pavlova does not so much imitate the movement of a butterfly as the emotional quality of a butterfly-flight, the sense raised in our minds by watching it." On November 4, 1911, after her first appearance in *L'Oiseau d'Or*, *The Times* again took note of this singular quality. "As in her famous 'Papillon' dance, so in 'L'Oiseau d'Or' her art is more suggestive than imitative. She does not copy a bird, but she seems for the moment to partake of its nature."

Resplendent in "a lemon-coloured tutu and orange corsage, and an audacious crest of scarlet and yellow ostrich feathers,"[1] Pavlova made her first appearance in *L'Oiseau d'Or* on November 3, 1911, at Covent Garden with Diaghilev's Ballets Russes. This "delightful little trifle"[2] (how Petipa would have winced) was none other than the Bluebird *pas de deux*, which had been inserted into *Le Festin* in Paris in 1909 and danced so brilliantly on that occasion by Karsavina and Nijinsky. In November 1911, with Karsavina in St. Petersburg, Pavlova had the chance to appear with Nijinsky in this virtuoso showpiece.

"Taken by itself it is little more than a display of the virtuosity of the two dancers," stated *The Times* the next morning. The critic then went on to qualify his statement, rhapsodizing over Pavlova's "pointed toe step," which he astutely noted "was used in a new way, with little clawing movements as though only a small thread held her to the ground and she were trying to free herself and sail away into mid-air."

Pavlova's ability to get under the skin of any character she played, and her inability to perform a step (even in a short virtuoso *divertissement)* without imbuing it with meaning, was observed by another critic: "Her every gesture and action was instinct with significance. . . . She invested her movements with a rare sense of suggestion. Of no other dancer can it be said that her performances are the ideal combination of music, dancing and acting."[3]

On November 11, 1911, Pavlova danced in *Le Pavillon d'Armide*, *Les Sylphides*, and *L'Oiseau d'Or*. It was her last appearance with Nijinsky and the Diaghilev company.

La Rose Mourante

It was inevitable that Pavlova and Diaghilev should part.[1] As Pavlova's genius would naturally outshine most of the dancers who would be present on the stage with her,[2] and make the standard of a ballet seem uneven, it is not surprising that audiences appreciated her solos more than they did her ballets. Pavlova's lack of affectation contributed to her success in this genre, for while other ballerinas would use their solos to show off their virtuosity, Pavlova would deliberately include only the simplest steps in hers.[3]

Both on and off the stage, Pavlova had a great affinity for nature. She had "a species of vision into the heart of things; a sensitiveness to what may be called the characteristic state of mind both of animate beings and inanimate things; and receptivity to those impressions which, interpreted into expression, enable Pavlova to endow flowers and birds and insects with lively and interesting sentiments."[4]

Pavlova's rendition of *La Rose Mourante* was a highly abstract work of art. It was not the physical aspects of the flower that she sought to represent, but the spirit of it with which she was in communion. Her deceptively simple costume sought to remind one of a rose, rather than to reproduce it. It was "purposely non-commital . . . designed to reveal movement, posture and line."[5]

Any other artist who danced *La Rose Mourante* in a flimsy costume of the palest pink, with a little pink rose-petal cap on her head, to the palm court music of Drigo's "Valse Bluette,"[6] may well have seemed ludicrous, as would have the rose's extreme freshness and lively last moments before its demise.[7] But Pavlova imbued a minor work with seriousness and charm.

(*above & left*) Studio portraits by Bransburg, London, c. 1911. Pavlova is not wearing the pink rose-petal chaplet that she wore in performance. The artificial roses were photographic props.

PART TWO

1912–1930

(*above*) As Amarilla. Studio portrait by Campbell-Gray, London, 1912. (*right*) With Novikoff and company, photographed on the stage of the Palace Theatre by Foulsham & Banfield, London, 1912.

Amarilla

Short, one-act ballet in which a passionate gypsy girl is compelled to dance at the betrothal festivities of the wealthy count who has spurned her love. Music by Glazunov, Drigo, and Dargomyzhsky; choreography by Zajlich; decor and costumes by Barbier. First performed at the Palace Theatre, London, on June 5, 1912, with Pavlova as Amarilla and Novikoff as Inigo; first seen in New York at the Manhattan Opera House on April 6, 1914.

"Amarilla" is not, in fact, very interesting. . . .There is rather too much pantomime.
The Times, London, June 6, 1912

In "Amarilla" . . . Pavlova remains the greatest dancing actress in the world.
New York Times, October 19, 1920

"Amarilla" was disgusting. . . . The scenery was unpleasant. . . . The gypsy girl of Pavlova was disagreeable: exaggerated, voluptuous, even hysterical. In a word, she was decadent.
Shin-Engei Magazine, Tokyo, October 1922

The setting is a lovely one, and the minuet danced by the entire company has a haunting melody. Anna Pavlova . . . was adorable, passionate and tender in turn, but always the embodiment of grace.
Statesman, Calcutta, January 9, 1923

As an actress she is not convincing, as anyone can convince himself by watching her critically in "Amarilla."
Sunday Times, London, September 14, 1924

It was all vivid imagery, in which the eminent dancer's gifts found the fullest expression.
Sydney Morning Herald, April 26, 1926

In "Amarilla" . . . Pavlova's power of mime was seen at its crowning zenith. . . . At the conclusion her facial gestures, limb movements and aimless flutterings conveyed a picture of tragic hopelessness that stirred the emotions to the depths.
New Zealand Herald, June 3, 1926

It is the dramatic quality of Pavlova's movements that makes her the great artist she is, for her least little gesture has a quality in it that is rarely achieved, and her exquisite lightness is a joy to watch.
Sphinx, Cairo, December 1, 1928

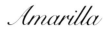

Amarilla

These photographs of Pavlova and Novikoff in *Amarilla*
were taken by Foulsham & Banfield on the stage
of the Palace Theatre, London, in 1912.
They were subsequently issued as a postcard set
in the Rotary Photographic Series.

(*above*) With Novikoff, posing on the Fern Walk at Ivy House. This photograph appeared on a full page in the *Tatler*, June 19, 1912, captioned "We Do Believe in Fairies." (*right*) Action photograph taken at the housewarming party. After leasing Ivy House in 1912, Pavlova eventually purchased it for £10,000 on November 17, 1914.

En Orange

Pas de deux with music by Giraud (orchestrated by Arends) and choreography by Gorsky. First performed at the Bolshoi Theater, Moscow, on December 4, 1911. Danced for the first time by Pavlova in the garden at Ivy House on the occasion of her housewarming party, June 13, 1912. Included in the repertoire of her 1913 season at the Palace Theatre, London, and first performed in the United States on her 1913–14 tour.

A bygone music hall ditty which was once in great favour sang the delights of the "Old Bull and Bush". The house which Mme. Pavlova has taken at Hampstead is just a little lower down the hill from that hostelry. From Golders Green station we climb to it by a road as steep as that which is stated, symbolically, to lead to heaven. And when Ivy House is reached it is indeed a paradise.

Era, London, June 15, 1912

Under the shade of a giant elm a number of silk-hatted and frock-coated gentlemen from the Palace orchestra discoursed sweet music. It is a pity they were not dressed in Lincoln green. Then the ensemble would have been complete. . . . Pavlova with her magic feet shod with gold, and fluttering draperies around her, flashed like a bright dream across the lawn, and danced a new delirious dance with her companion Novikoff. The touch of barbaric splendour was marvellously realised by Novikoff with his rough fur robe and his astonishing muscles. *Daily News*, London, June 14, 1912

When Pavlova herself danced out of the screen of evergreen in a waving orange robe, everybody, from the Duchess of Marlborough on the lawn to the housemaids peeping out of the top window, clapped till the garden rang.

She danced "Un Orange" [*sic*] with a Corin in sheepskin, falling into his arms, running away from him and falling sobbing to the ground, with her head veiled in folds of orange and gossamer: then peeping out to show him that she was only laughing all the while. It was a dance that the Bacchanals themselves could not put in the shade, and one of the subtlest fascinations was the pause here and there when the music and Pavlova and her shepherd—and, it seemed, the very birds and boughs— stood still.

It showed how little Pavlova depends on all the wonderful "effects" which the Palace Theatre weaves around her dances; that, on her own lawn, with only Nature as stage-manager, she should have held her guests so spellbound. *Daily Express*, London, June 14, 1912

Coquetterie de Colombine

Pas de trois with music by Drigo and choreography by the Legat brothers, an excerpt from *The Fairy Doll*. First performed in London on April 15, 1912, at the Palace Theatre, with Pavlova, Novikoff, and Chiriaieff, and in New York on November 3, 1913, at the Metropolitan Opera House, with Pavlova, Novikoff, and Bergé.

It was a gala night on Monday, when the most fascinating of all the Tsar's fascinating dancers made her reappearance in London. A great storm of applause swept the house as she stepped before the foot-lights, and when, her dazzling programme completed, she stood bowing her acknowledgments, she was absolutely embowered in the costly flowers that had been showered upon her. I have never seen any more bewitching performance than Pavlova's "Coquetterie de Colombine," which was one of the new numbers she favoured us with. M. Novikoff and M. Chiriaieff divided the honours as Harlequin and Pierrot, and between them fluttered the dainty Pavlova in a spirit of charming capriciousness, treating each of her companions in turn to the witchery of her smiles. Pavlova doesn't only dance the part; she acts it with all the accomplished art of a great actress, and just the right little touch of comedy is added at the end, when the dancer lures the Harlequin and his rival to her side, and slips away at the last moment to leave them embracing one another instead of her.   *Umpire*, Manchester, April 21, 1912

Those who know Pavlova can guess how bewitching she is in such a part. . . . She is grace and delicacy personified. How she flirts! With what charming grace does she play off one lover against the other! And how she dances! A feather does not look any more airy than she. Thistledown, blown hither and thither in the breeze.   *Tatler*, London, May 15, 1912

When at last Pavlova herself appeared as the Colombine in that enchanting Pas de Trois . . . the house shook. It was soon seen that the evening was going to be one of her great ones.
          Pall Mall Gazette, London, August 5, 1912

(*above & left*) As Colombine. Photographs by Mishkin, New York, 1913.

New Gavotte Pavlova

The third of a series of social dances created in the summer of 1914 to music especially composed by Jacoby and orchestrated by Schmidt, with choreography by Clustine and costumes by Rothenstein. These photographs of Pavlova and Clustine were taken in London by Elwin Neame prior to Pavlova's departure for America, where *New Gavotte Pavlova* was first performed on November 2, 1914, in Bridgeport, Connecticut, on the opening night of her 1914–15 tour.

The Dumb Girl of Portici

Pavlova's only feature film, "A Great Motion Picture Spectacle based on Auber's Famous Opera *Masaniello*," in which she portrayed the dumb girl Fenella. Adapted, produced, and directed by Lois Weber. Produced at the Universal Studios, Universal City, California, and Chicago. Released by Universal Film Manufacturing Co., 1916.

"Ever since I was old enough to know what the stage meant I have been possessed by a desire to play the role of Fenella."—Pavlova   Unidentified clipping, dated 1916, Dandré press file

The advent of Pavlova in the second decade of the twentieth century as an exponent of the silent drama is surely the greatest conquest the youthful art has achieved and is of far greater significance than the mere visualization of her terpsichorean genius.

Souvenir program, first London showing at the Philharmonic Hall, May 10, 1916

The Russian celebrity is the only woman in all the world who could portray the role which has frightened more singers and caused more of a furor in its day than any mind of an author has ever conceived. It is as Fenella that Pavlova will electrify the world.

Publicity leaflet for Broadway presentation

The whole affair must be judged the most remarkable blending of picture skill and acting effort that the films have known.   *Cleveland Plain Dealer*, May 3, 1916

Pavlova Got $66.66 Per Minute Appearing as Movie Actress   *Denver News*, April 9, 1916

With the fortune she earned in making "The Blind Girl of Portici" [*sic*] for the Universal, she went out one day and purchased the Boston Grand Opera Company. Truly a lady of courage and enterprise.
Los Angeles Times, January 7, 1916

Pavlova is not a woman—she is an experience. As "The Dumb Girl of Portici," on view all week at the Alhambra, you may not like her at first, but slowly and surely she will crawl into your heart and almost break it when at last you see her soul winging through the clouds and almost hear her whisper—"Do you remember?"
Cleveland Leader, April 30, 1916

(*above*) As Fenella. Photograph by E. Hutchinson, Chicago, 1915.   (*left*) Film still reproduced
as a souvenir postcard in the "Pictures" Portrait Gallery Series, London, 1916.

(above & right) As Aurora. Photographs by Mishkin, New York, 1916.

The Sleeping Beauty

Abridged version of the Petipa–Tchaikovsky classic, restaged by Clustine, decors and costumes by Léon Bakst. First presented in Charles Dillingham's *The Big Show* at the New York Hippodrome, August 31, 1916. Originally in four tableaux, the lavish production was gradually depleted to a fifteen-minute *divertissement* by the end of its run on January 20, 1917.

It has long been Mlle. Pavlova's desire to remain permanently in New York and to present ballet performances as dignified and as artistic as those in Paris and Petrograd.

Musical America, New York, August 10, 1916

"I remember that Dillingham production; I should remember it. It was called *The Big Show* and it was BIG. There were Power's elephants, Mooney's horses, a trained lion act. Then came Pavlova in *The Sleeping Beauty* with Bakst's settings. And after Pavlova came the Mammoth Minstrel Show with a cast of 400—count 'em—400. Oh, the dear, dead wonderful Hippodrome." — Sol Hurok

Impresario (London, 1947)

A more beautiful ballet than this lavish and at the same time exquisite production has never been seen in New York. . . . Regal splendor was followed by a moonlit vision of nymphs no less than enchanting, and the awakening of the Princess was celebrated by a festival that reached its height when white-robed creature[s] with intertwining garlands were drawn high into the air to make a living frame for a stage picture such as is seldom seen. . . . Altogether this ballet was fascinating in its movement and dazzling in its splendor. It set a new artistic standard for the Hippodrome.

New York Evening World, September 5, 1916

At the Metropolitan Opera House the same dancing would have created a furore. The apathy of the great crowds which found so much to delight them in other features of "The Big Show" must have been a great disappointment to her, but she was philosophical enough to recognize that she was dancing in the wrong place. She persevered until her contract was fulfilled and did not once complain. The real eccentricity of Pavlova's genius is her self-discipline.

New York World, January 21, 1917

(*above & right*) Two of the Hill Studios series of photographs that created a sensation in the New York press in December 1916.

Dragonfly

Solo to Kreisler's "Schön Rosmarin," choreography by Pavlova, costume of blue, green, and purple net designed by Pavlova. This brief vignette, a brilliant study in allegro, was conceived during Pavlova's visit to St. Petersburg in 1914 and was performed by her on the first night of her season at the Century Opera House, New York, February 2, 1915. Introduced into the *divertissements* in *The Big Show*, November 27, 1916. First performed in England at the Theatre Royal, Drury Lane, April 15, 1920.

Anna Pavlova, première danseuse at the Hippodrome, made a complete change in her divertissement yesterday evening, and "The Sleeping Beauty" is no more. It was replaced by a program of request numbers. . . . Last night Mme. Pavlova danced in the "Dragon Fly," music by Kreisler, and in the "Gavotte Pavlova," music by Lincke, assisted by Volinine.   *New York Telegraph*, November 28, 1916

How Pavlova has taken the lead for dancing photography—as for everything she touches! Her series of poses that have been switched upside down, sideways or at odd angles—to represent flying and floating in midair—are astounding. Absolutely astounding perfection of pose and body. . . .   *New York Review*, December 30, 1916

Before your very eyes the wings flashed and flamed, the lithe body quivered, almost still, then darted on a new caprice. Tier on tier, the dim audience, with not a gap in the ranks, held its breath in a bewitched silence. Suddenly, in a corner at the back of the stage, Pavlova's foot slipped. Should we have noticed had it been anyone else? Perhaps not. It was so small a slip—the ball of the foot seemed to slide along an excessively planished surface, for just the space of a heart-beat out of control. Instantly through the vast audience went a sound as though the wind had suddenly lifted the arms of spellbound trees. It was a sound of sheer surprise, forced out by the incredible. Pavlova's foot had slipped!   *Manchester Guardian*, October 30, 1925

"Pavlova in her Dragonfly Dance gave the impression of being even more fleeting and swift than a real dragonfly."—Sir Frederick Ashton   In conversation

Gavotte

Pas de deux to Lincke's "Glowworm," choreography by Ivan Clustine, Directoire dress of lemon satin, trimmed with black velvet, designed by Serge Oukrainsky. The embodiment of gaiety, this *divertissement* almost equaled *The Swan* in popularity and remained in Pavlova's repertoire until the end of her life. First performed as *Gavotte Directoire* by Pavlova and Marcel Bergé at the Metropolitan Opera House, New York, November 3, 1913, and first seen in London on October 12, 1914, at the Palace Theatre.

Pavlova captivated her audience with her divertissements. The celebrated "Pavlova Gavotte" danced with Monsieur Vajinski was continuously applauded from the moment the graceful pair appeared and until the last step and genuflexion had been given.　　　*St. Louis Globe-Democrat*, January 4, 1922

The principal item was an exquisitely graceful dance in Directoire costume by Mme. Pavlova herself, with M. Volinine. It was delightful to note what fresh interest and charm such graceful movements gave to the old melody of the "Glow-Worm."　　　*Statesman*, Calcutta, January 21, 1923

In the final set of divertissements, Pavlova substituted her "Gavotte" for the announced "Serenade," and the applause was thunderous as her poke bonnet appeared round the curtain. For this Frenchy dance she wore a lemon gown, which would make even Paris sit up and take notice. The dance's simplicity, brought out by the queen of dancing, was its beauty. . . . Yes, the great Pavlova has plenty of pep with which to give us another farewell tour in a couple of years.
　　　Omaha News, February 12, 1925

Her first dance caused a hurricane—and so it went on till a climax was reached in something like an earthquake after she had danced the Pavlova Gavotte with M. Volinine.
　　　Daily News, London, September 9, 1925

The audience "went wild" over a gavotte, danced by Mme. Pavlova in a Directoire dress which indicated that women's clothes had been venturesome and "slinky" a long time before 1925.
　　　Daily Mail, London, September 9, 1925

With a delightful old world grace that quite melted the heart, Pavlova, robed in yellow satin with a long train caught at her waist and wearing a demure poke bonnet, gave new insight into her extrovert personality.　　　*New Zealand Herald*, May 31, 1926

(*above & left*) With Volinine. Photograph above by C. Rivas, Mexico City, 1917; action photograph at left by *The Times*, taken at the Royal Opera House, Covent Garden, 1923.

Gavotte

Pavlova and Volinine in *Gavotte* were perennially favorite subjects of photographers all over the world. These photographs were taken (1) by Dubreuil in Lima in 1917, (2 & 3) by Mishkin in New York in 1916, and (4) by Monte Luke in Sydney in 1929.

(2)

(1)

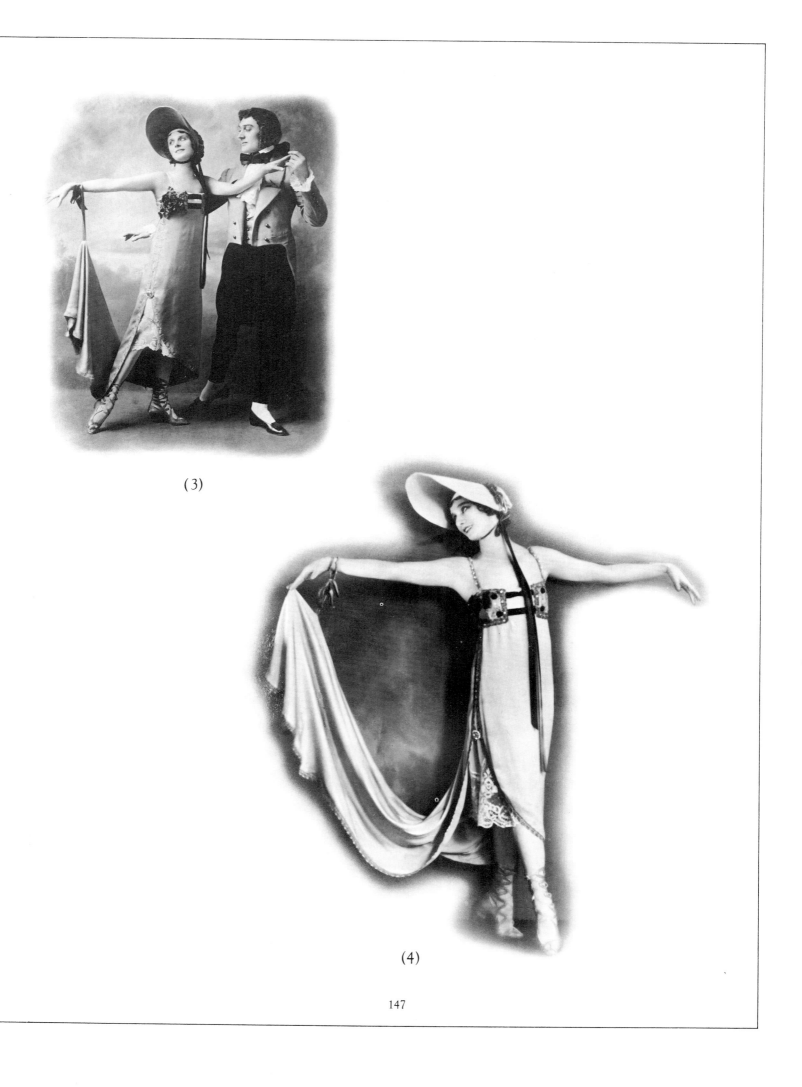

(3)

(4)

Petite Danse Russe

Traditional Russian peasant dance performed by Pavlova and eight couples, with music by Dvořák and choreography by Clustine. First given in London on October 12, 1914, at a special matinee in aid of the Red Cross at the Palace Theatre.

Photograph by Abbe, c. 1916.

Pas de Trois

Pas de trois with music by Godard, choreography by Clustine, and costumes by Oukrainsky. First performed by Pavlova, Oukrainsky, and Bergé at the London Opera House on October 6, 1913, and at the Manhattan Opera House on November 19, 1913.
Photograph by Van Riel, Buenos Aires, 1918.

Les Préludes

One-act choreographic poem by Fokine after Lamartine's *Méditations Poétiques*, with music by Liszt and decor and costumes by Boris Anisfeld. First performed by the Pavlova company at the Kroll Opera House, Berlin, January 15, 1913; opened Pavlova's 1913 season at the Palace Theatre on April 21; first performed in New York on November 3, 1913, at the Metropolitan Opera House. Although never popular with audiences, either in England or America (where in the program it was subtitled *A Futuristic Ballet*), Pavlova kept it in her repertoire until 1925.

The dancing . . . is carried out by a bevy of gauzy creatures, presumably embodiments of youth and joy, whose charming revels are overshadowed by the apparition of dark-apparelled and mysterious beings (who may represent Fate and the unknown). M. Anisfeld's scenery and dresses (the scenery bizarre, the dresses all airy webs) are engaging and show Mme. Pavlova to have concerned herself with matters in which, now and then in the past, she did not quite do her radiant self justice.

Daily Mail, London, April 22, 1913

Perhaps the most elaborate spectacle which Mme. Pavlova has yet presented in England. Both as regards the settings and the costumes it was a strange mixture of the wholly charming and the quaintly grotesque, which occasionally suggested that Herr Boris Anisfeld . . . had fallen under the Futurist influence. But of the dancing . . . there could be no two opinions.

The Times, London, April 22, 1913

The dances show Mlle. Pavlova in her finest mood. She has given us no subtler, no more appealing expression of the hopes and yearning which lie too deep for tears or joy. If it is the highest achievement of dancing to conjure up those *états d'âme*, which words avail nothing to describe and no words can compel, this is dancing at its greatest.

Daily Telegraph, London, April 22, 1913

This proved the least successful number of the day, as the result of trying to "interpret" absolute music in terms of pirouettes pleased neither those who enjoy pirouettes nor those who have enjoyed the music as an unviolated poem. The scenery for this dance was apparently in futuristic style and succeeded in taking attention away from the dancers while the audience tried to puzzle out what it all meant.

New York Times, November 4, 1913

(*above*) As the Spirit of Love. Photograph by Van Riel, Buenos Aires, 1917.
(*left*) With Novikoff and company, posing on stage. This photograph was reproduced in the souvenir program for her 1913–14 U. S. tour.

Walpurgis Night

Ballet in one act and two scenes from Gounod's *Faust*, with choreography by Clustine, decor by Sime, and costumes by Kalloch and Oukrainsky. First performed by Pavlova and Alexandre Volinine at the Metropolitan Opera House, New York, on November 24, 1914, at a special benefit for the Red Cross. The ballet was performed in *Faust* when the Pavlova company appeared with the Century Opera Company (Chicago, 1914), the Boston Grand Opera Company (1915–16), and the Colon Opera Company (Buenos Aires, 1917).

Chicago has not seen the Walpurgis night scene before so far as I have been able to discover. Mephistopheles in a desperate effort to make Faust forget Marguerite offers him as a sop all the notorious beauties of history. The scene originally included a chorus of flying witches.

   As it was presented last evening, Henry Weldon spoke the magic word and up went a curtain revealing not a cleft in the rocks nor a palace but one of the most gorgeous recesses of a forgotten, ruinous city. Mephistopheles, transformed to an animated clay image, was the only diabolical figure in the picture. Mlle. Pavlova finally revealed herself, not as Helen of Troy, but as herself, and everyone, I think forgot the opera.   *Chicago Tribune,* December 22, 1914

The second part of the programme was devoted to the one-act ballet from the opera *Faust,* arranged by Ivan Clustine, which created a fantastic effect evocative of ancient times. The magnificent scenery, dramatic lighting effects, brilliant dancing and period costumes all made a wonderful impression on the public.   *Illustrated Daily,* Santiago, July 20, 1917

An introductory setting in which Faust and Mephisto appeared led to a tableau of figures in classical Grecian and Egyptian garb, posed strikingly in a fine picture of a mountain fastness—the Brocken scene idealised and presenting the appearance . . . of some great gallery painting. Here, enthroned on the Harz Mountains, was Helen of Troy and her attendant court. . . . Madame Pavlova, as Helen, danced with irresistible grace, and her satellites moved with beautiful effect in a stage-picture of entrancing tones.   *Sydney Morning Herald,* April 26, 1926

(*above & left*) As Helen of Troy. Studio portraits by Dubreuil, Lima, 1917.

Invitation to the Dance

One-act ballet to Weber's *Aufforderung zum Tanz* (op. 65), with choreography by Zajlich and costumes by Walter. A shy young debutante attends her first ball. First performed in London on June 10, 1913, at the Palace Theatre, and in New York on November 17, 1913. Revived for Pavlova's 1925 season at the Royal Opera House, Covent Garden, with new decor by Nicholas Benois and costumes by Barbier.

Photograph by Dubreuil, Lima, 1917.

Christmas

Romantic *divertissement* arranged by Pavlova, Clustine, and Volinine to Tchaikovsky's "December Waltz." An eighteenth-century coquette flirts and dances with five cavaliers at a Christmas party. Finally she puts on a down-trimmed pink taffeta cloak, bonnet, and muff and vanishes into the night with her true love. Date of creation uncertain. First performed in England on April 26. 1920, at Drury Lane.

Photograph by Baron de Meyer, c. 1920.

Raymonda

Two-act version of Petipa's ballet, including the birthday scene and the dream sequence, with music by Glazunov, choreography by Clustine, and costumes by Kalloch. First performed on the opening night of Pavlova's season at the Century Opera House, New York, February 2, 1915, with Pavlova as Raymonda and Volinine as the Crusader.

Except for a certain effectiveness of costuming which goes with the period of thirteenth-century France, there is little of note in the new ballet that differs from most of the others in which Pavlova has been seen. The scenario has little power to hold itself, and there are dull and characterless stretches in the music which was not particularly well played last night. Nevertheless opportunities for the display of the principal dancer's talents and those of certain members of her company are not lacking, and this was what the audience was most interested in.   *New York Times,* February 3, 1915

In "Raymonda," the new Clustine-Glazunov pantomime ballet, Pavlova exhibits every type of art from realistic tragedy to the most superficial of mincing steps.   *New York Evening Mail,* February 3, 1915

Those who were present at the Coliseo last night certainly saw the world-renowned troupe of dancers at their very best. Glazunov's music in "Raymonda" is so wholly in agreement with the action of the story, the clever use of harps and horns to convey the atmosphere of the "dream" which occupies the whole of the second act is so entirely in accord with one's idea of what dream symphonies ought to be, that individual criticism of the several parts of the ballet is almost impossible. Pre-eminent was the bewitching pas-seul by Mlle. Pavlova accompanied on the harp alone, and the quartet immediately following was also worthy of note.   *Buenos Aires Herald,* August 24, 1917

A romantic story, an enchanted garden, a moonlit night, and marvellous music. Such is "Raymonda." . . . The interpretation of the ballet by Anna Pavlova and her company is superb. The choreography, the second-act scenery and—above all—the music make this the best ballet she has given us to date.
                        Mercurio, Santiago, July 26, 1918

(*above*) As Raymonda. Photograph, c. 1915.   (*left*) With Volinine as the Crusader.
Photograph by C. Rivas, Mexico City, 1917.

Orpheus

One-act ballet from Gluck's *Orpheus*, with choreography by Clustine and decor and costumes by Urban. First performed in Chicago in October 1915, when it was included in performances of Gluck's opera during Pavlova's appearances with the Boston Grand Opera Company. First given in New York at the Manhattan Opera House on October 26, 1915, and in London at the Theatre Royal, Drury Lane, on May 10, 1920, on the same program as *La Péri*.

From Gluck to Paul Dukas is indeed a very far cry, and it may well have been a desire to present an extraordinarily piquant contrast that induced Madame Pavlova last night to preface the production of "La Péri," a dance poem, as it was described, the music of which is by the French composer, with an "Orpheus" ballet based upon Gluck's famous opera. Certainly it would be hard to imagine a more striking contrast in styles from every standpoint, choreographic as well as musical. The scene in the Elysian Fields—not too happily conceived pictorially, and far too bright, to our thinking, in the lighting—gave us Grecian poses and classic graces, and some very exquisite dancing, as poetical as the heart could desire, from Pavlova herself, aided and abetted in one dance by the accomplished M. Volinine. There are ballets in the present repertory that afford Pavlova's magical art greater and more varied scope, but what it gives her to do is done with all the witchery and charm of which she holds the secret.

Daily Telegraph, London, May 11, 1920

In this version there is little suggestion of drama. . . . A succession of movements expressively danced, a stage setting by no means too ethereal for Elysium, and occasional appearances of the incomparable Pavlova herself; that is all. It is perhaps inevitable that in productions designedly arranged for a *primissima ballerina* the *ensemble* will suffer. Pavlova fills the stage as much when it is crowded as when it is empty, and the details suffer. But the tunes were very good, and conscientiously played throughout under M. Stier. And Pavlova was certainly Elysian.

The Times, London, May 11, 1920

(*above*) Studio portrait by Strauss Peyton, Kansas City, c. 1916.
(*left*) The photograph Bakst used as the sideturned silhouette in the souvenir program of *The Big Show*.

La Péri

One-act choreographic poem with music by Dukas,
choreography by Stowitts and Clustine, and decor and
costumes by Stowitts. First performed at the Teatro Coliseo,
Buenos Aires, August 1917. Opened Pavlova's one-week
season at the Manhattan Opera House, New York,
on October 18, 1920, at a special benefit performance
for the Manhattan Navy Club. Pavlova posed in her exotic
green and gold costume with Hubert Stowitts for these
photographs taken (1–3) by Van Riel in Buenos Aires
in 1919 and (4) by Abbe in New York in 1920.

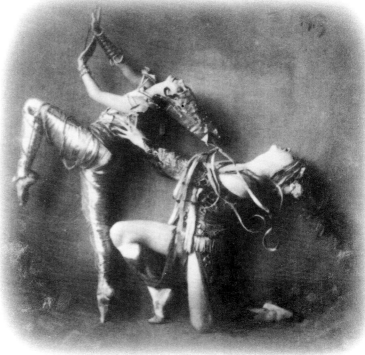

(2)

(1)

(3)

(4)

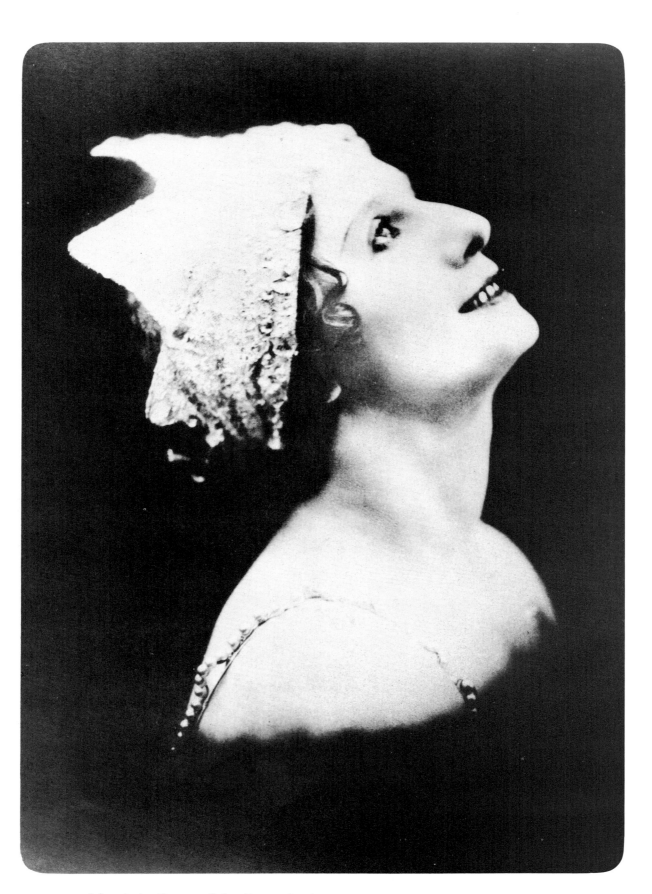

(*above*) As Queen of the Snow. Studio portrait by Dobson, Liverpool, 1921.
(*right*) With Volinine. Photograph, c. 1920.

Snowflakes

One-act ballet derived from the snowflake scene in Act 1 of Tchaikovsky's *Nutcracker*, with choreography by Clustine, decor by Urban, and costumes by Korovin. First performed in Chicago in October 1915 during Pavlova's appearances with the Boston Grand Opera Company. Opened Pavlova's London season at the Theatre Royal, Drury Lane, April 12, 1920.

Snowflakes, by Ivan Clustine, is a dull and heavy thing to fasten on to little "Casse-Noisettes"; but it does give Mme. Pavlova the chance of proving that she is still absolute mistress of the technical "stunts" of her art.
The Times, London, April 13, 1920.

Mme. Pavlova's second appearance at the Manhattan last night drew a great audience, that greeted with delight the famous artist's entrance, midway in the program in a Russian classic, Tschaikowsky's "Snowflakes" from the Nutcracker ballet. Lightest of all the human snowflakes was Pavlova herself, as her flashing flights and poses, sudden revolutions and marvelous rests, suggested the glancing facets of a diamond.
New York Times, October 20, 1920

The exquisite "Snowflakes," from Tschaikowsky's "Nutcracker Suite," proved to be one of the daintiest and most atmospheric of all the ballets danced here, and every principal as well as the ensemble excelled in its interpretation. The scenery, costuming and lighting were exceptionally artistic.
Milwaukee Telegram, January 18, 1925

Pavlova herself was most delicate of the snowflakes. She fluttered more slowly than the others, like a lonely flake seeking a resting place at the beginning or end of a storm, or like a perfect crystal standing out in a cloud of blown snow. The other snowflakes dashed about madly in whirls and eddies. Pavlova's every movement was precise—she was the gem in a whirl of white.   *Omaha News*, February 12, 1925

The scene suggested a fairyland winter in its half-lights tinted with purple; and Madame Pavlova suddenly appeared like a fairy queen in the midst of the revels. . . .
Sydney Morning Herald, May 3, 1926

Pavlova gave her work the certain touch of poetic beauty, sweeping aside all antecedent and contemporary technique by a perfection quite unparalleled.   *New Zealand Herald*, May 31, 1926

Snowflakes

These photographs of Pavlova in *Snowflakes* were
taken by Abbe in his New York studio during her season
at the Manhattan Opera House in the fall of 1920.

(*above*) Studio portrait in costume for *Diana Mexicana*.
(*right*) With Domyslawski in the same dance. Photographs undated.

166

Mexican Dances

A set of three traditional Mexican dances (*China Poblana, Jarabe Tapatio,* and *Diana Mexicana*), with libretto by Jaime Martino del Rio, music by Manuel Castro Padilla, and decor and costumes by Adolfo Best-Maugaro. The dances, some of which were classicized to include pointwork, were taught to Pavlova and her company by local teachers; the scenery, music, and costumes were presented as a gift from the people of Mexico City, where *Mexican Dances* was first performed. Opened Pavlova's season at the Prince's Theatre, London, June 15, 1920. First performed in New York at the Manhattan Opera House on March 10, 1921.

The first number, "China Poblana," is named after "the Chinese Girl of Pueblo," a character of ancient Mexican history . . . . A strong Chinese influence is notable in Mexican textile art works, embroideries, laces, pottery and metal works. Such oriental feeling is apparent in the quaintly beautiful costumes worn in this number. "Jarabe Tapatio" is a characteristic dance form peculiar to the natives of a certain region in the state of Jalisco and environs of the city of Guadalajara. The third and last number, "Diana Mexicana," is named for a familiar Mexican folk melody of rapid, fortissimo movement and buoyant rhythm employed by the composer in this typically Mexican dance.

Souvenir program for Pavlova's 1920–21 U.S. tour

The Mexican dances which she brought to the Prince's Theatre on Tuesday shock one at first, because they are so unlike what she has hitherto done, and it is startling to hear her feet making noises on the stage just like the feet of common women. But whatever she does, whether she clothes herself like a Mexican cowboy or puts on the conventional dress of a ballet-dancer, she is altogether adorable.

Observer, London, June 20, 1920

These dances revealed a mixed ancestry one naturally expected from tunes of such origin. . . . But it was less easy to account for the Dutch flavouring of one of Madame Pavlova's numbers. Delightfully quaint were her movements both in that and another dance—and extraordinarily becoming the national costume she wore—while the last dance of all proved as jolly and exhilarating a thing you could wish to see, and her performance of it a pure joy in its complete realisation of that mood.

Daily Telegraph, London, June 17, 1920

167

Giselle

Clustine's version of the two-act ballet to music by Adam
with decor by Urban. The ballet remained in Pavlova's
repertoire until 1930 and was immensely popular
with audiences everywhere. Although Pavlova's Act 1
costume was traditional (based on the 1908 Bakst design),
for Act 2 she wore a free-flowing dress of white crepe
georgette, in which she posed with Volinine for
this series of photographs taken by Abbe
in New York in 1920.

The Fauns

One-act choreographic poem by Clustine with music by Ilia Satz and costumes by N. Remisoff and R. Kalloch. Created for the Fête de Nuit à Bagatelle in the Bois de Boulogne, Paris, June 21, 1921, with Pavlova as the Bacchante and Bergé and Stowitts as the two Fauns. First performed in America on November 1, 1921, during Pavlova's two-week season at the Manhattan Opera House. Dropped from her repertoire after her 1922 tour of Japan.

Mme. Pavlova surprised her warmest devotees of dancing at the Manhattan last night . . . with a novelty unlike any she has ever given before. It was a wild "goat dance" of sheer animal spirits that the veteran Clustine devised to a flute and horn duet of hollow consecutive fifths, orchestrated into something like "music" by Ilia Satz, with a stageful of dancers, men and women, completely disguised in goatskin costumes designed by Remisoff, scenic artist of the Maryinsky Theatre in Petrograd. "The Fauns," as the piece is called, had no relation to its post-prandial namesake composed by Debussy. It is a mad bacchanale . . . recalling the diabolic pranks of Nijinsky years ago on this same stage in the "Till Eulenspiegel" of Strauss.

Mr. Novikoff as the Young Faun was enough to dispel any rumors that "they do this 'barer' in Paris," where the daring "tableau symphonique" was first staged at the Parc des Bagatelles last June. Pavlova herself was the solitary maiden, captured by the riot of faunal creatures, carried on shoulders this way and that, and swept away in the crowd as a gust scatters Autumn leaves, vanishing even before a quick curtain.
New York Times, November 2, 1921

Last of the novelties was "The Fauns" presented for the first time on Tuesday night's program. It brought forward some interesting music by Ilia Satz, and a beautiful setting of tall trees against a red-hued sky, but in action it is merely episodic. Fauns gamboled without much choreographic method, and one particular faun, impersonated with remarkable effect by Mr. Nelle, displayed some persistence in his pursuit of a beautiful nymph known to spectators as Pavlova.
Musical America, New York, November 12, 1921

(*above*) Posing in the garden at Ivy House in the summer of 1921. Photograph by H. N. King.
(*left*) With Novikoff, posing on the stage of the Manhattan Opera House in the fall of 1921.
Photograph by Abbe.

Russian Dance

A lively Russian peasant dance to Rubinstein's arrangement of Tchaikovsky's "Danse Russe" from *Swan Lake* and a traditional folk melody, with choreography by Clustine and decor and costumes by Serge Soudeikine. First performed in Quebec, October 15, 1921.

With its striking post-impressionist set, for which the brushes of Soudeikine ran riot; with its bizarre painted costumes, and with Pavlova as its central figure, a coquettish, merry peasant, it was as successful in New York as in the old Canadian city.   *Musical America,* New York, November 12, 1921

Pavlova and M. Algeranoff appeared in the final brilliant number, a Russian dance to music by Rubinstein-Tschaikowski. It was a spectacular dance in which the dancers wore wonderful Russian costumes of the brightest colors.   *El Paso Times,* May 4, 1925

The program closed with a Russian dance, in which "the incomparable" cavorted about like a girl in her teens, with nary a sign of fatigue, nothing apparent but joy in motion.
Omaha News, February 12, 1925

The scenery was fascinatingly picturesque, showing a grotesque country scene in Russia, with some wooden peasant huts, a rustic bridge, and a huge rainbow in the sky. Eight Russian girls in brightly coloured costumes formed a background for the solo dancers. . . . Mr. Algeranoff, in a vivacious Russian trepak, danced at an amazing pace in a sitting position, and brought down the house with his unique technique and manly vigour. Anna Pavlova made a strikingly beautiful picture in her magnificent costume and headdress, and acted with fascinating and roguish coquetry, evading the young peasant's advances, who was encouraged to press on his suit by the other girls. This dance was superbly executed by both dancers, and completely captivated the audience.   *Sydney Mail,* April 27, 1926

(*above*) Posing in Abbe's New York studio, 1921.
(*left*) Action photograph by *The Times*, London, 1923.

Egyptian Ballet

One-act ballet to music by Luigini, Verdi, and Arensky, with choreography by Clustine, decor by Samoiloff, and costumes by Bilibin. First performed in 1917 during Pavlova's tour of South America. Given on the 1920–21 U.S. tour, with Marie Oleonova in the leading role. Performed in 1923 in Cairo, where the ballet, with Pavlova, had a great success. Pavlova and Novikoff posed for these publicity photographs by Hoppé in the garden at Ivy House in 1923.

(*above*) As the Fairy Doll. A rare backstage photograph by Abbe, 1923.
(*right*) With Pierre Vladimirov, backstage. Photograph by Yaravoff, Montevideo, 1928.

The Fairy Doll

Clustine's version of the Legat brothers' ballet in one act and two scenes, with music by Bayer, Rubinstein, and Drigo and decor and costumes by Mitislav Dobuzhinsky. First performed by Pavlova and Volinine at the Metropolitan Opera House, New York, on November 24, 1914, at a special benefit for the Red Cross, and seen in London for the first time on June 24, 1920, at the Prince's Theatre. Presented with new decor and costumes by Soudeikine at the Royal Opera House, Covent Garden, September 10, 1923.

There is Pavlova herself, light as a breath of air, pirouetting marvellously, so dainty as to make the stage a very temple of delight. . . . The dolls show off their specialities, representatives of the Allied nations come in (bearing a delicate tribute in the shape of small Argentine flags) and the ballet ends in a grand march. It is as pretty, as pleasing, and as graceful an entertainment as one could devise for artists and children of all ages, and makes one think regretfully of the airs and graces of the olden time, and of what the English pantomime has lost by woeful lack of imagination.

Buenos Aires Herald, August 15, 1917

Here is a creature of incredible grace. Even when motionless she is a picture of physical elegance. . . . For a time in the opening ballet, "The Fairy Doll," she stood marshalling the throng of puppets with a magic wand, with barely perceptible motions of the arms and of her lovely, infinitely plastic hands. This, together with the changes of her bewitching, expressive face, was a revelation of the fine art of posture.

St. Louis Post-Dispatch, January 3, 1922

Its only fault is that it reminds us too much of *La Boutique Fantasque*, without the originality in grouping and movement which made the peculiar brilliance of that production, and without the music.

The Times, London, September 11, 1923

If it is not particularly original, it does not matter; it gives us Pavlova at her best . . . a delightful ballet that one would like to see more often. It seemed to go better on Saturday than before. But perhaps the world has forgotten "La Boutique Fastasque"—or never seen it.

Morning Post, London, September 22, 1924

The Fairy Doll

These photographs of Pavlova and Volinine,
in the *grand adage* from the second scene of *The Fairy Doll,*
were taken by a photographer from *The Times* during
performances at the Royal Opera House,
Covent Garden, in September 1923.

Ajanta's Frescoes

Ballet in one act and four scenes, inspired by Pavlova's visit to the Ajanta caves in Hyderabad. Specially commissioned score by Alexander Tcherepnin, choreography by Clustine, decors by Allegri, and costumes by Solomon. Presented on the opening night of Pavlova's 1923 season at the Royal Opera House, Covent Garden, September 10. First performed in America on October 15, 1923, at the Manhattan Opera House, New York.

In "Ajanta's Frescoes" Mme. Pavlova has tried to reproduce the vitality of the frescoes at Ajanta, in India, a great Buddhist temple. The pilgrims enter the temple and fall asleep, and the frescoes unroll themselves and play a great drama of 2,500 years ago. It is a scene of great beauty of colour and the weirdest dances danced to the weirdest of music.   *Daily News,* London, September 11, 1923

If there is any criticism to be made it is that in the dances, and more especially in Mme. Pavlova's own dancing, too many of the *clichés* of the conventional ballet make their appearance.
                                                        The Times, London, September 11, 1923

Mr. Novikoff is the Prince Gautama who, sated with a life of perpetual ballet, leaves the exhausted dancers with a gesture of heroic relinquishment and takes to the religious life. Mme. Pavlova dances the traditional measures which, when executed with her peculiar spirit and intensity, suit any time and clime, and there is a real Oriental dance performed by two fantastically slim Indians.
                                                        Daily Mail, London, September 23, 1924

Glittering phantasmagoria of tinted forms amid which Pavlova darted like an embodied flame, made a climax of "Ajanta" comparable to the best stagecraft of exotic ballet by Russian masters of the art. It was the woman's triumph as stage manager no less than as dancer, in music as in costume original and daring.

   Through outer and inner veils of India's historic, rock-carved temples, the rising scenes gave dissolving view of worshippers prone before dim altars. Later in a reverse cycle, the temple walls closed on the vision of a princely Buddha, recoiling from earthly orgy to higher contemplation. Few ballets have so suggested the Emersonian epigram "Ralph, this is Poetry."—"Margaret, it is religion."
                                                        New York Times, October 16, 1923

(*above*) With Novikoff. Photograph by Abbe, 1923.
(*left*) Action photograph by *The Times*, London, 1923.

Japanese Dances

The first of three miniatures, one Japanese and two Hindu, which comprised *Oriental Impressions,* the ballet inspired by Pavlova's visit to the East. With decor by Allegri and music by Henry Geehl from an original Japanese theme, the three Japanese dances (*Dojoji, Kappore,* and *Takesu Bayashi*) were arranged by Pavlova under the direction of Fijima and Fumi, dance professors in Tokyo. During the summer of 1923 Pavlova, wearing her own kimono, posed on the lawn at Ivy House for this series of photographs by Hoppé.

(*above*) As Radha. Portrait by Hoppé, London, 1923.
(*right*) With Uday Shankar. Photograph by Stephenson Studios, Atlanta, 1923.

Krishna and Radha

The first of the two Hindu miniatures in *Oriental Impressions* was *A Hindu Wedding*, representing a traditional ceremony. The second, *Krishna and Radha,* was based on a Hindu folk dance. Both dances, performed in authentic Indian costumes, were arranged by Uday Shankar to music by Comolata Banerji. The decor, copied from old Hindu miniatures, was by Allegri. *Oriental Impressions* was premiered at the Royal Opera House, Covent Garden, on September 13, 1923, and in America on October 9, 1923, at the Manhattan Opera House, New York.

The two British India bits that completed the novel "Oriental Impressions" were arrangements by Miss Comolata Banerji of cleverly devised dances and drumbeats of striking effect, though drawn from quite customary Western orchestration. . . . Pavlova in her new production, like Chaplin directing his ideal picture, has achieved a work of creative imagination, with the visual truth possible only to a great executant artist.
New York Times, October 10, 1923

Krishna was the Orpheus of the Indies and in the next ballet—danced by Uday Shankar—he played the flute beneath a turquoise blue flood. . . . Pavlova, as Radha, floated on the scene in raspberry red and yellow. She was the incarnation of the god Krishna's song.
New York Morning Telegraph, October 10, 1923

In the Indian dance, . . . she reached a height of tragic intensity which only a great artist, as well as a great dancer, could have attained. The whole of this miniature, in the grouping of the ballet, the colour scheme of the dresses, and the lighting was beyond praise.
Morning Post, London, September 12, 1924

Madame Pavlova herself appeared in "Krishna and Radha." After a bevy of maidens in long coloured veils had circled round the god, and had laid at his feet offerings of fruit and flowers, Radha came in wearing a robe with a long pink skirt, and set herself to charm him with a dance. . . . A striking and very beautiful feature of this dance was the way it emphasised the undulatory movements of the arms and hands, which paused at intervals to freeze themselves into some conventional pose that delighted the eye with its flowing grace of line.
Sydney Morning Herald, April 22, 1929

(*above*) As Kitri, in Act 1.   (*right*) As Dulcinea, with Novikoff as the Knight of the Silver Shield in Act 2.
Photographed by Abbe on the stage of the Royal Opera House, Covent Garden, September 1924.

Don Quixote

Novikoff's staging, in two acts, three scenes, and prologue, of the old Minkus ballet, with decor and costumes designed by Korovin. The prologue and first act adhered to the Moscow Gorsky version, but the staging of the second act was entirely original and incorporated passages of music not in the original score. Opened Pavlova's 1924 London season at the Royal Opera House, Covent Garden, on September 8. First performed in America on October 17, 1924, at the Manhattan Opera House, New York.

A thunderous roar went up when first she stepped on to the stage in the "Don Quixote" ballet. Her pirouettes and sylph-like leaps in the air evoked tempests of hand-clapping. Sometimes the orchestra was drowned and the progress of the ballet stopped while the audience indulged its frenzy of delight. When the curtain fell after each successive act there were recalls on recalls. There seemed no end to this rapture. People in the stalls fell back, fatigued with applauding.

Daily News, London, September 9, 1924

The enthusiasm at Covent Garden last night was a tribute to what great technique can do. When the curtain fell on "Don Quixote" and rose again to display an array of bouquets that would have stocked a florist's shop, the house was beside itself. *Morning Post,* London, September 9, 1924

Pavlova danced like a golden butterfly into the view of a great audience of her worshippers at Covent Garden last night. . . . Infected by her soundless art and swayed by the magic of her lyrical movements, the audience scarcely dared breathe. *Daily Mail,* London, September 9, 1924

They say that Pavlova will return no more. The thought is almost terrifying, for one is averse to the idea of ever being deprived of so much loveliness. . . . Her dancing is one of the glories of the world. She still remains "the incomparable," aloof, soaring above her companions to an exalted height, where she shines splenderously. *Indianapolis News,* January 6, 1925

Last night every part of the theatre was packed; people stood three or four deep round the dress circle, and when the famous dancer tripped on in the "Don Quixote" ballet . . . a storm of cheering greeted her. . . . Recall followed recall at the end of the first part of the ballet, . . . the scene at this point resembling a great garden, so many were the floral tributes in the foreground.

Sydney Morning Herald, May 21, 1926

Don Quixote

Pavlova's costumes for the 1924 production
of *Don Quixote* were delayed en route from Paris.
For this set of publicity photographs, taken by Hugh Cecil
in London, Pavlova posed (1–3) in her *Souvenir d'Espagna*
costume and (4) in the Spanish Doll's costume
from her production of *The Fairy Doll.*

(2)

(1)

(3)

(4)

Dance of the Hours

Ballet sequence from Ponchielli's opera *La Gioconda*, arranged by Clustine. In this short *divertissement* Pavlova and her partner were supported by a *corps de ballet* of twelve girls representing the hours. First performed in the United States c. 1915 with Pavlova and Volinine. Photograph by Schneider, Berlin, c. 1925, of Pavlova in her Korovin-designed costume of gold and yellow tarlatan.

Californian Poppy

Solo to Tchaikovsky's Melody in E Flat with choreography and costume by Pavlova. The dance depicted a day in the life of the spectacular Californian poppy, which closes its petals at sunset. Created c. 1916 in the United States and first performed in England at the Theatre Royal, Drury Lane, on April 26, 1920. Photograph by Becker & Mass, Berlin, c. 1925.

An Old Russian Folk Lore

One-act ballet based on the traditional folk tale "The Enchanted Bird–Princess," to a specially commissioned score by Nicolas Tcherepnin, with choreography by Novikoff and decor and costumes by Bilibin. First performed with Pavlova as the Enchanted Bird–Princess and Novikoff as Ivan Czarevich on September 17, 1923, at the Royal Opera House, Covent Garden. Opened Pavlova's season at the Manhattan Opera House, New York, on October 8, 1923, with the emended title *Russian Folk Lore*.

To the old King Dodon from "Coq d'Or" with his astrologer and four new black cats and a further retinue out of "Petrushka," the thistledown heroine danced in fresh guise, first as the "Firebird's" fluttering [s]elf, and finally as a silver-ikon imaged bride. It was Pavlova's gesture to a vanished Russia of Slavic romance and Tartar fairy tale and so was recognized and applauded.

New York Times, October 9, 1923

"An Old Russian Folk Lore" reminds the audience at point after point of "Petrouchka," "Firebird" and "Le Coq d'Or." No doubt, the literary themes of these ballets are old ones, that have been handled in many forms, and it is incorrect to say that Mme. Pavlova's versions of them are founded on Diaghileff's. But the public does not make these fine distinctions because it has not the necessary historical knowledge. It knows only that its first acquaintance with these subjects was through Diaghileff's ballets, and that the corresponding features in the Pavlova ballets merely look like inferior treatments of Diaghileff's dances.

Glasgow Herald, October 20, 1925

There can be no objection to this recasting of familiar material; for folklore is common property. But it is unfortunate that the treatment of it should be so like what we have seen infinitely better done before. Of the music the same may be said; there was little in the score that has not been better done by Rimsky-Korsakov and Stravinsky.

The Times, London, October 13, 1925

Pavlova here is first enchanted bird, then humanised, and we discover that she is most human when enchanted, and most enchanting when she is human.

Daily Telegraph, London, October 13, 1925

(above) Studio portrait as the Enchanted Bird – Princess.
(left) With Novikoff as Ivan Czarevich. Photographs by Andrew, New Zealand, 1926.

Chopiniana

Suite of dances set to Chopin piano pieces orchestrated by Glazunov. Choreography by Clustine (with the exception of the Waltz in C Sharp Minor, by Fokine) and decor by Pazetti. First performed (as *Une Soirée de Chopin*) at the London Opera House on October 6, 1913, and (as *Une Soirée de Danse*) at the Metropolitan Opera House, New York, on November 3, 1913. Remained in Pavlova's repertoire until the end of her life. These photographs of Pavlova and Pierre Vladimirov were taken (1) by Ross Verlag in Berlin in 1928, (2 & 3) by Yaravoff in Montevideo in 1928, and (4) by S. P. Andrew in Auckland in 1926.

(2)

(1)

(3)

(4)

Dionysus

Ballet in one act and two scenes, with choreography by Clustine, music by Nicolas Tcherep-nin, decor and special lighting effects by Nicolas de Lipsky, and costumes by Soudeikine. First performed, with Pavlova as the High Priestess and Novikoff as Dionysus, at the Manhattan Opera House, New York, on November 4, 1921, and at the Royal Opera House, Covent Garden, on September 13, 1923. One of her few successful esoteric ballets.

Lipsky lights and a Pavlova impersonation, among the Russian dancer's best, in the new "Dionysus" at the Manhattan last evening, stirred the largest audience of this week's ballets to a popular ovation recalling the old-time opera "riots" when Oscar was consul. The seven-veiled star enacted with fine dignity the pagan priestess of a pre-Volstead age, whose lonely vigil before the Greek god's shrine was suddenly and magically turned into a vision of a Tanagra vase figure dancing a fantasy-nocturne bac-chanale.

New York Times, November 5, 1921

It is only when Pavlova comes smiling before the lowered curtain that one realizes the fullness of her own triumph. . . . Not only for its scenic wonder-making was "Dionysus" the chief of Pavlova's novel-ties. The Tcherepnin music for the ballet was of more than usual interest, fitly evoking the tonal atmosphere for the art of the dancer.

Musical America, New York, November 12, 1921

What Pavlova can make of such a part is easier to imagine than to tell adequately. Certainly there was not a gesture that did not show that incomparable grace that is the hallmark of her genius. Her first leap to the more urgent call of the music of the love scene was in itself a wonderful thing—the very embodiment of youth, of energy, of life that throbs to the rhythm of the Spring.

Daily Telegraph, London, September 14, 1923

Before the eyes of the audience, as Dionysus stepped from his pedestal, the rocky bluffs disappeared, and the setting suddenly became a sylvan garden on the shores of a lake, beneath hanging branches of tall trees. . . . A similar process has already been employed here in some of the musical comedies or revues. . . . But these alterations were of a fugitive character as compared with that of Saturday night, where the whole scene was changed by the mere timing of an electric switch.

Sydney Morning Herald, May 10, 1926

(*above*) As the High Priestess, with Novikoff as Dionysus.   (*left*) A group from the ballet.
Photographs by Yaravoff, Montevideo, 1928.

Rondino

Solo to a variation on a theme of Beethoven by Kreisler, with choreography and costume by Pavlova. Created c. 1916 in the United States as *Rondo,* the choreography of this stately dance originally featured byplay with a lorgnette; this was later replaced by a huge ostrich-feather fan, which at the end of the dance Pavlova used to conceal herself from an imaginary suitor. First seen in England at the Theatre Royal, Drury Lane, on April 19, 1920. Photograph of Pavlova in her mauve tarlatan dress by Becker & Mass, Berlin, c. 1928.

Au Bal

Divertissement to Tchaikovsky's mazurka from the last act of *The Sleeping Beauty*, with choreography by Boris Romanov and costumes by Leon Zack. In this comic vignette, occasionally billed as *Blue Mazurka*, a coquette invited, only to refuse, the advances of six young officers at a ball. First performed during Pavlova's last season at the Royal Opera House, Covent Garden, September 1927. Photograph of Pavlova in her elaborate blue and silver costume and plumed hat by Becker & Mass, Berlin, c. 1928.

(*above*) As Lise, in Act 1. Photograph by Yaravoff, Montevideo, 1928.
(*right*) With Novikoff as Colin. Photograph by Schneider, Berlin, 1926.

La Fille Mal Gardée

One-act version of the Petipa–Ivanov staging of Dauberval's ballet with music by Hertel, choreography credited variously to Chiriaieff and Zajlich. First given at the Palace Theatre, London, on July 15, 1912, with Pavlova as Eliza (i.e., Lise) and Novikoff as Colin. Extended two-act version first seen in New York at the Manhattan Opera House on April 15, 1914, with the same cast. Revived with new decor by Allegri at the Royal Opera House, Covent Garden, on September 19, 1923. Pavlova did not dance the lead role in this revival in London until September 16, 1927, during her last season at the Royal Opera House.

Mme. Pavlova changed her programme last night in order to give what she always gives—herself. Her admirers can desire no more. The ballet "La Fille Mal Gardée" allows her scope to be herself. That is its merit. *The Times*, London, September 17, 1927

The moment Pavlova came on the stage in "La Fille Mal Gardée" (Precaution in Vain) . . . the sombre gold and pink surroundings of the Opera House faded into the beyond. We forgot the dismal weather and saw only the wonderful artist dancing in the sunshine and green fields and surrounded by her laughing, happy guests in the prettiest clothes imaginable. *Daily Mirror*, London, September 17, 1927

Of course, Mme. Pavlova was the centre of interest. Fortunately she was on the stage practically from the rise to the fall of the curtain. And it is interesting to see her in a part in which miming is as important as dancing. She is mistress of the one as much as of the other. When she coquettes with her lover, or when she cajoles her stern parent, she fascinates just as surely as when she performs feats of dancing with such perfect grace. *Daily Telegraph*, London, September 17, 1927

"La Fille Mal Gardée" is rather a conventional old ballet. . . . Pavlova, who danced the leading part at the revival last night at Covent Garden, was neither a village girl nor was she the least bit conventional. A joyous tropical bird among a flock of sparrows! That was the impression she left. This curiously vivid creature was alive and original every moment. It was a long ballet, and Pavlova was on stage nearly the whole time, but she never lowered her pitch. *Evening News*, London, September 17, 1927

(*above*) As the Chrysanthemum, with Volinine as the Poet. Photograph by Abbe, New York, 1920. (*right*) With Aubrey Hitchins as the North Wind. Photograph by Van Riel, Buenos Aires, 1928.

Autumn Leaves

One-act choreographic poem by Pavlova set to Chopin piano pieces orchestrated by Hinrichs, Bowden, and Schmidt. Premiered in South America c. 1919 with decor by Aravantinos. Presented with new decor and costumes by Korovin on May 3, 1920, at the Theatre Royal, Drury Lane, and on October 20, 1920, at the Manhattan Opera House.

More New Yorkers wished to see Mme. Pavlova yesterday than the Manhattan Opera House could hold in two performances, afternoon and night, some 7,000 attending the pair of them. The evening bill brought a novelty in the week's series, "Autumn Leaves," . . . in which she portrayed a chrysanthemum buffeted by the breeze, rescued and then cast away by a poet's hand.

New York Times, October 21, 1920

Before a crowded audience, which included the countess of Lytton, Madame Pavlova made her final bow to the Calcutta public at the Empire Theatre yesterday afternoon. . . . The heartiest applause was reserved for such classical favourites as "Autumn Leaves."   *Statesman,* Calcutta, January 24, 1923

One of the best ballets seen at Covent Garden during the present season was given last night by Mme. Pavlova. . . . Best, because more homogeneous and because in it Mme. Pavlova's supreme skill finds an outlet in a style that suits her completely.   *The Times,* London, October 20, 1925

Madame Anna Pavlova made a great feature last night at the Theatre Royal of her own beautiful setting of "Autumn Leaves." . . . The imagery of this scene captivated all beholders. . . . Madame Pavlova danced with the utmost beauty as the Chrysanthemum. *Sydney Morning Herald,* May 2, 1929

Pavlova comes all too rarely to Scotland. . . . At the Alhambra this week the world-famous danseuse presents a programme which is quite unparalleled in theatrical circles. . . . Of all the items presented "Autumn Leaves" . . . is easily the best. . . . In his personification of the wind Mr. Hitchins is amongst the most effective of the masculine dancers, and Pavlova, the flower which he breaks off and tosses aside, is splendidly forlorn.   *Glasgow Weekly Herald,* November 22, 1930

Finale

The fragile Chrysanthemum, stripped of its petals by the relentless North Wind, is torn from the arms of the Poet. Taken in November 1930 on stage at the Alhambra Theatre in Glasgow, this is probably the last photograph of Anna Pavlova in performance. It is appropriate that the ballet was Pavlova's own creation to music of her favorite composer, Chopin. Valerian Svetlov believed that *Autumn Leaves* "contained the whole psychology of her creative work and the prophecy of her tragic fate."

On December 8 Pavlova began a one-week season at the Hippodrome in the London suburb of Golders Green. Alicia Markova and Frederick Ashton were in the audience at the mid-week matinee, and after the performance they went backstage to see Pavlova. Markova says she will remember to the end of her life that last meeting with the woman who inspired her career, while Ashton still cherishes Pavlova's last words to him. She clasped his hand and said, "You have a great future. It will come slowly, but it will come."

Arnold Haskell, who watched the same performance from the wings, remembers the tumultuous applause that followed *The Swan.* "I looked up, and she still looked a very young girl while the applause was going on. . . . Then the curtain clanged down, and suddenly she became very old and tired the minute that contact with the public had been cut off." The importance of the reciprocal relationship between Pavlova and her audience was recognized by Haskell, as it had been by his friend and mentor, Svetlov, at the beginning of her career.

When the curtain fell on December 13, the last night of the Hippodrome season, no one knew that Pavlova had given her final performance.

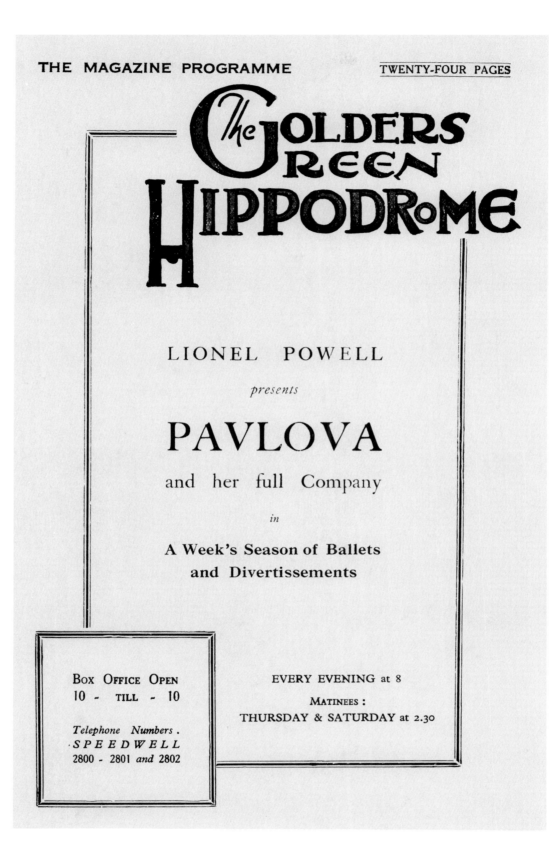

The GOLDERS GREEN HIPPODROME

LIONEL POWELL

presents

PAVLOVA

and her full Company

in

**A Week's Season of Ballets
and Divertissements**

BOX OFFICE OPEN
10 - TILL - 10

Telephone Numbers .
·*SPEEDWELL*
2800 - 2801 *and* 2802

EVERY EVENING at 8

MATINEES :
THURSDAY & SATURDAY at 2.30

(*above*) Program of Pavlova's last performance, at the Hippodrome, Golders Green. She danced in *Amarilla*, *Gavotte*, *The Swan*, and the *grand pas classique* from *Paquita*.
(*left*) In *Autumn Leaves*, with Hitchins and Vladimirov, posing on the stage of the Alhambra Theatre, Glasgow, November 1930. Photograph by the *Daily Record*, Glasgow.

Notes

Debut (page 24)

1 Fantastic ballet in one act to music by Richter, first produced on April 3, 1891, for the examination performance in the school theater. The ballet was never included in the Maryinsky repertoire.

2 The performance was a benefit for Anna Johansson, daughter of the celebrated dancer and teacher Christian Johansson. Kchessinskaya made her debut as Aspicia at this performance.

3 This girl, a classmate of Pavlova's, was the most promising pupil at the school. Her career was brilliant but brief, as she was dogged by ill health. She died at the age of thirty-six.

4 Petipa's third daughter, known in the company as Petipa III, was also a classmate of Pavlova's. She was a gifted pupil with exceptional elevation. However, she married and retired after only one season at the Maryinsky.

5 Valerian Svetlov, "Pavlova: Poet of the Dance," in *The Dance Magazine*, New York, August 1931.

Giselle (page 26)

1 This was the fifth appearance Pavlova had made at the Maryinsky since *Daughter of the Pharaoh* on October 21, 1898. She had appeared twice in the *pas de quatre* in *The Halt of the Cavalry* and twice in *La Fille Mal Gardée*, once in the *pas de six* and once in the *pas de trois*.

In the spring of 1899, Pavlova danced in the *pas de quatre* in *The Halt of the Cavlary* on April 10, the night before her graduation, and on April 21, at a benefit for the *corps de ballet*. She appeared in the *pas de six* in *La Fille Mal Gardée* on April 28. The next morning the *Petersburgskaya gazeta* noted that "the pupil Pavlova stands out for her grace, softness, and femininity. Her dancing produces . . . an impression of elegance and lack of affectation." The reviewer concluded that she could be considered to have reached the grade of soloist "on the strength of this performance alone."

The following autumn Pavlova danced in the *pas de trois* in *La Fille Mal Gardée*. Her performance on September 19, 1899, which marked her debut as a member of the Maryinsky company, provoked the following comment from the *Petersburgskii listok*: "Pavel Gerdt's school was reflected to the fullest degree in the dancing of his pupils. Belinskaya's speed and Pavlova's airiness, lightness, and marvelous grace give one reason to hope that in time these pretty girls will make excellent dancers."

2 Alexander Pleshcheyev, *Pod seniyou kulis* (Paris: Maison du Livre Etranger, 1936).

3 André Levinson, "Anna Pavlova," in *Solntse Rosii*, St. Petersburg, 1913, No. 1.

4 Valerian Svetlov, "Tsaritsa Mab," in *Ogni*, St. Petersburg, 1906, No. 3.

Esmeralda (page 28)

1 The occasion was a benefit for N. S. Aistov, principal regisseur of the Imperial Ballet at the Maryinsky from 1889 to 1904. Kchessinskaya made her debut as Esmeralda at this performance.

2 Pavlova's variation gave her the chance to display her remarkable *ballon* and to execute a brilliant series of pirouettes. Both Pavlova and Petipa received warm receptions from the audience and were highly praised by the critics, although several noted an element of competition. "Pavlova II and Petipa III, who performed the friends of Fleur de Lys, vied with each other, as it were, during the dancing, so much effort did they display. In all fairness, the latter gained the greater victory." (Clipping from Pleshcheyev's press book.)

Harlequinade (page 31)

1 Ballets bearing alternative French titles in the Imperial Theaters repertoire fell into three categories: (1) Russian ballets first performed at the court theaters, such as the Hermitage Theater and the Peterhof Palace Theater, (2) ballets first produced in France and later restaged in Russia, such as *La Fille Mal Gardée*, *La Vivandiére*, and *Le Corsaire*, and (3) ballets based on French stories or themes, such as *La Belle au Bois Dormant* and *Barbe-bleue*.

2 Among Kchessinskaya's monopoly ballets were *Daughter of the Pharaoh*, *Esmeralda*, and *La Fille Mal Gardée*.

3 Pavlova made her debut as Columbine in Berlin in 1908.

4 Pavlova made her debut as Pierrette on January 25, 1902, at the Hermitage Theater.

Bluebeard (page 32)

1 Pavlova danced several roles in this ballet. On September 3, 1900, she made her debut as Anna, performing the Fin de Siècle Polka with such fervor and aplomb that it was encored to tumultuous applause. On September 17 she played both Anna and Venus. The *Petersburgskaya gazeta* noted the next day that Pavlova's Anna was not completely successful technically but had to admit that "the young artist made one forget the faults of the previous acts by her graceful performance as Venus."

The Sleeping Beauty (page 33)

1 Of the five roles in *The Sleeping Beauty* that were eventually included in Pavlova's repertoire, Florine was best suited to her talent and temperament. She had danced the Fairy Candide (a.k.a. Lily of the Valley, Wildflower, Carnation, Crystal Fountain, et al.) in 1899 but had great trouble in mastering the solo. Because of her weak feet, the sustained pointwork of the variation was very difficult for her. Petipa sternly made her rehearse it time and again. Several years later, in 1903, she danced the Canary Fairy (a.k.a. Songbirds et al.). Although she was by then technically stronger, she fared little better in the brief but taxing variation, based entirely on runs on point. By the time Pavlova made her debuts as Aurora and the Lilac Fairy in 1908—on January 6 and February 16, respectively—she was an accomplished technician, but she found little to interest her in either role. The Lilac Fairy was soon dropped from her repertoire, and Aurora, the role that had inspired her childhood ambition, proved to be less than ideal for the mature dancer. Svetlov, who witnessed her debut as Aurora, said that the role eluded her. Pavlova did subsequently dance Aurora with success, notably at the New York Hippodrome in

1916, but she was never an academic dancer and was thus never entirely in sympathy with the role. Interestingly, in more recent years both Galina Ulanova and Natalia Makarova have expressed similar sentiments.

The Awakening of Flora (page 34)

1 Valerian Svetlov, *Terpsichore* (St. Petersburg: 1906).

2 Only five months earlier, on April 26, 1900, Pavlova played the secondary role of Aurora to Lubov Petipa's Flora.

3 The ballet was first staged at the Peterhof Palace Theater on July 28, 1894, with Kchessinskaya in the leading role.

4 Sergei Khudekov, in *Petersburgskaya gazeta*, October 8, 1901. The powerful Khudekov, publisher and editor of the paper, was an enemy of Petipa and a staunch supporter of Kchessinskaya. He always reviewed her performances in glowing terms.

5 As reported by Svetlov in *Terpsichore*.

King Candaule (page 36)

1 Collection of clippings from Pleshcheyev's press book, dated but untitled.

2 It was a historic occasion: Nijinsky made his first appearance of the season in the *pas de deux* of the Mulatto and the Bayadère in the second act's *grand ballabile lydien*. Together with Aspicia's hunting scene in *Daughter of the Pharaoh*, this was one of the most spectacular *pas* ever mounted on the Maryinsky stage.

Camargo (page 38)

1 Ballet in three acts and eight scenes, with a libretto by Saint-Georges and Petipa, music by Minkus, and choreography by Petipa. Set in the period of Louis XV, *Camargo* was first produced for the benefit of Adele Grantzova on December 17, 1872. The following year a revised version by Ivanov, in three acts and five scenes, with decors by Allegri, was mounted for the benefit of Ekaterina Vazem.

The Magic Flute (page 42)

1 On the same evening Pavlova danced the Queen of the Naiads in *Sylvia*.

2 Pavlova was nevertheless very fond of *The Magic Flute* and later mounted her own version, aided by Cecchetti. Her version was premiered at the London Opera House on October 7, 1913, with Pavlova as Lise, Laurent Novikoff as Luke, and Cecchetti as the Marquis. It was first seen in New York, with the same cast, at the Metropolitan Opera House on November 3, 1913.

3 As told to the authors by Tamara Karsavina.

4 *Petersburgskaya gazeta*, January 1, 1902.

The Magic Flute (page 44)

1 Kchessinskaya's monopoly on *La Fille Mal Gardée* was broken by Preobrajenskaya on January 15, 1906. On the same evening, in Moscow, Pavlova made her debut in *Daughter of the Pharaoh*. Hardly a coincidence.

Javotte (page 46)

1 Michel Fokine, *Protiv techeniya* (Leningrad and Moscow: Iskusstvo, 1962).
2 Michel Fokine, "Michel Fokine Remembers," in *The Dance Magazine*, New York, August 1931.
3 Pavlova created the role of the Vine Spirit and performed a *pas de deux* with Fokine.
4 Pavlova created the role of Actea on February 10, 1907. In the spring of the same year she made her debut as Eunice at the Hermitage Theater, Moscow, where excerpts from the ballet were performed on May 25. She did not dance this role at the Maryinsky until February 16, 1908.

Carmen (page 49)

1 Such as the intermezzo "The Faithful Shepherdess" in Act 2 of *The Queen of Spades*, the polonaise and mazurka in Act 2 of *A Life for the Tsar*, the lezghinka in Act 2 of *The Demon*, the lezghinka in *Russlan and Ludmilla*, the waltz in *Der Freischütz*, and the gypsy dances in *Russalka*. Pavlova performed in all of these except *The Queen of Spades*.
2 Quoted from Vera Krasovskaya, *Russkii baletnyi teatr nachala XX veka*, vol. 2, *Tantsovshchiki* (Leningrad: Iskusstvo, 1972).
3 The dances were first choreographed by Petipa for a performance of *Carmen* on October 29, 1882. The choreography was revised by Cecchetti in 1885. But the Olé, as danced by Pavlova, was kept as Petipa had originally set it.

The Demon (page 50)

1 Korovin's costumes were so successful that they remained in use until the 1940s.

Raymonda (page 52)

1 Pavlova never performed the leading role in Russia. Preobrajenskaya, the ballet's most celebrated interpreter, held a monopoly on it until 1910, when it was inherited by Karsavina.

La Bayadère (page 53)

1 The ballet is performed at the Kirov today in three acts. Act 4 was dropped in 1919, and its *pas d'action* was transferred to Act 2. The ballet ends with the Kingdom of the Shades scene. The production mounted by Natalia Makarova for American Ballet Theatre in 1980 is also in three acts, but it follows the story line to its original conclusion. The final act shows the wedding of Gamzatti and Solor and the resulting vengeance of the gods in the destruction of the temple. In an apotheosis the spirits of Nikiya and Solor are united as she leads him upward into an afterlife.
2 Of Pavlova's performance on January 21, 1901, Alexander Pleshcheyev wrote, "Pavlova flew across the stage." (*Novoye vremya*, St. Petersburg, January 22, 1901.) Another critic later wrote, "Pavlova's appearance, with her sweeping, remarkably light and elegant flight in the 'Shades,' provoked a storm of applause. The whole theater applauded as one man. Of course, the artists had to dance an encore." (*Petersburgskii listok*, September 12, 1902.)

La Bayadère (page 55)

1 Previous interpreters of the part were Vazem (1877), Johansson (1884), Kchessinskaya (1900), and Geltzer (1901). After considerable persuasion Kchessinskaya bequeathed Nikiya to Pavlova and even helped Sokolova to coach Pavlova for the role. Vazem, Sokolova, Kchessinskaya, and Grimaldi all shared a box in the theater on April 28, 1902, when Pavlova made her debut as Nikiya with Pavel Gerdt as Solor. Such is the strength of tradition in the Russian ballet, carried through to the present day: when Nadezhda Pavlova made her debut as Giselle at the Bolshoi Theater in Moscow, in 1975, three generations of great Russian Giselles were present.
2 André Levinson, "Anna Pavlova," in *Solntse Rosii*, St. Petersburg, 1913, No. 1.
3 This myth has been perpetuated by the film *The Immortal Swan*, compiled after Pavlova's death. Recorded experimentally on silent film in Hollywood, and elsewhere, in 1924–25, the dance sequences were later dubbed with a musical soundtrack. Although most sequences are effective, one sequence (of *Rondino*, filmed in Australia in 1929) is totally misleading: the first section of the dance is speeded up, the last section is in slow motion, and the music is in no way related to either.
4 Pavlova used similar timing in the mad scene of *Giselle* and in *The Swan*. Levinson believed that this "disintegration of the rhythm" was an essential aspect of Pavlova's stagecraft.
5 Levinson, "Anna Pavlova."
6 Ibid.

La Bayadère (page 57)

1 In the version given at the Kirov today this is the second scene of Act 1.

The Fairy Doll (page 58)

1 *Die Puppenfee*, a comic ballet in one act, with a libretto by Hassreiter and Gaul, music by Bayer, and choreography by Hassreiter, was first performed in 1888 in Vienna.

2 His designs for the ill-fated 1901 production of *Sylvia* were never used. Petipa's *Le Coeur de la Marquise*, a ballet pantomime first produced on February 22, 1902, at the Hermitage Theater was Bakst's first realized commission for the ballet—and for the theater.

3 Additional pieces of music by Rubinstein and Drigo were interpolated into the score for the Legat brothers' production. The *pas de trois* to Drigo's music was to become well known in the West as *Coquetterie de Colombine*.

4 Nicolas Legat, in "As Friends Recall Her," a collection of reminiscences in *The Dance Magazine*, New York, August 1931.

Coppélia (page 60)

1 Pavlova never danced Swanilda at the Maryinsky. The first Maryinsky ballerina to perform the role was Varvara Nikitina in 1884, followed by Kchessinskaya in 1894, Preobrajenskaya in 1897, and Trefilova in 1900. Pavlova made her debut as Swanilda on June 6, 1907, at the Hermitage Theater, Moscow, with Mikhail Obukhov as Franz.

The Magic Mirror (page 61)

1 Petipa personally rehearsed Pavlova in the part. He recorded in his diary on the night of the premiere that the ballet was a "fiasco" and that the music, decors, and costumes were "hideous."

Giselle (page 62)

1 At the turn of the century *Giselle* was not popular in St. Petersburg and was usually put on for visiting ballerinas, who were expected to perform at least one virtuoso variation to music of their choice. Pavlova was only the seventh Russian *Giselle* to appear on the St. Petersburg stage since the ballet's first performance there in 1842. The others were Andreyanova (1842), Bogdanova (1856), Muravieva (1862), Vazem (1878), Gorshenkova (1884), and Preobrajenskaya (1899).

2 *Petersburgskaya gazeta*, August 26, 1911. Quoted from Vera Krasovskaya, *Russkii baletnyi teatr nachala XX veka*, vol. 2, *Tantsovshchiki* (Leningrad: Iskusstvo, 1972).

3 Valerian Svetlov, "Tsaritsa Mab," in *Ogni*, St. Petersburg, 1906, No. 3.

4 Tamara Karsavina, "Anna Pavlova," in *Slavonic Review*, London, March 1931.

5 *Birzhevyi vedomosti*, St. Petersburg, May 1, 1903.

6 Valerian Svetlov, *Terpsichore* (St. Petersburg, 1906).

7 Petipa's diary for November 1, 1904, reads, "Pavlova came to see me, so that I could go through the 'mad scene' in *Giselle* with her tomorrow." Quoted from *Marius Petipa: Materiali, vospominanya, stati* (Leningrad: Iskusstvo, 1971).

8 *Petersburgskii dnevik teatrala*, November 18, 1904.

The Naiad and the Fisherman (page 66)

1 Jules Perrot's ballet *Ondine* was restaged by Petipa on October 27, 1874, at the Bolshoi Theater, St. Petersburg, retitled *The Naiad and the Fisherman*.

2 Valerian Svetlov, *Terpsichore* (St. Petersburg, 1906).

3 Valerian Svetlov, quoted from Vera Krasovskaya, *Russkii baletnyi teatr nachala XX veka*, vol. 2, *Tantsovshchiki* (Leningrad: Iskusstvo, 1972).

4 Valerian Svetlov, in *Petersburgskaya gazeta*, December 8, 1903.

5 Pavlova was granted leave of absence from May 20 to September 20, 1903, to study with the celebrated teacher.

6 Alexander Chiriaieff supervised this revival of Petipa's ballet, but Petipa himself arranged a new *pas de deux* especially for Pavlova.

7 Collection of clippings from Pleshcheyev's press book, dated but untitled.

Le Corsaire (page 69)

1 The first staging of the ballet in Russia was on January 12, 1858, in a revised version by Jules Perrot, with an additional *pas d'esclave* choreographed by Petipa to music by Oldenbourg.

2 The critic of *Novosti* praised Pavlova's remarkable *ballon* in the first act and her brilliant variation in "Le Jardin Animé" and noted that "of all the participants, Pavlova had the biggest success." At this performance she also appeared in the *pas d'esclave*, a *terre à terre* dance that, as one reviewer remarked, "was not at all suitable for her type of talent. This artist flutters and flies, but in the *pas d'esclave* she did not leave the ground."

Paquita (page 70)

1 Valerian Svetlov, *Terpsichore* (St. Petersburg, 1906).

2 *Petersburgskaya gazeta*, May 3, 1904.

3 Both variations were choreographed especially for Pavlova by Petipa.

4 Svetlov, *Terpsichore*.

5 Alexander Pleshcheyev, in *Novoye vremya*, St. Petersburg, October 26, 1904.

Le Corsaire (page 73)

1 This scene was considered by several contemporary critics to be in bad taste. Karsavina, in conversation with the authors, disagreed, contending that it was one of the high points of the ballet.
2 Valerian Svetlov, *Terpsichore* (St. Petersburg, 1906).
3 Valerian Svetlov, in *Birzhevye vedomosti*, St. Petersburg, December 7, 1904.
4 A variation in Act 2 performed *en travesti*.
5 Roslavleva had died at the tragically young age of thirty, only twelve days before Pavlova's debut in *Le Corsaire*.
6 Alexander Pleshcheyev, in *Petersburgskaya gazeta*, December 6, 1904.
7 "Le Jardin Animé," a masterpiece of symphonic choreography at the end of Act 3, was choreographed by Petipa for a revival of the ballet at the Bolshoi Theater, St. Petersburg, on January 25, 1868.
8 Valerian Svetlov, in *Birzhevye vedomosti*, St. Petersburg, December 7, 1904.
9 Unidentified clipping from Pleshcheyev's press book.

Don Quixote (page 74)

1 Vladimir Teliakovsky, director of the Imperial Theaters, had invited Gorsky to mount his successful Moscow production of *Don Quixote* in St. Petersburg. Premiered on January 20, 1902, with Kchessinskaya as Kitri, it was the first production on the Maryinsky stage by a Moscow ballet master during Petipa's reign. Pavlova danced Juanita, the fan seller, and the last-act fandango with Georgi Kiaksht to music especially composed by Eduard Napravnik. She did not begin to dance Kitri until nearly four years later, but, once she did, she met with universal critical acclaim. The glowing press notices of her performances at the Maryinsky would fill a fair-sized volume in themselves.

Daughter of the Pharaoh (page 77)

1 The production was first given in Moscow on November 27, 1905.
2 *Russkoye slovo*, quoted in Vera Krasovskaya, *Anna Pavlova* (Leningrad and Moscow: Iskusstvo, 1965).

Le Pavillon d'Armide (page 82)

1 Alexandre Benois, *Memoirs*, vol. 2 (London: Chatto & Windus, 1964).
2 Valerian Svetlov, in *Birzhevye vedomosti*, St. Petersburg, November 4, 1908.
3 Akim Volynsky, in *Zhizn iskusstva*, Petrograd, May 15, 1923.
4 Pavlova and Nijinsky first performed together on January 24, 1906, in *Roses and Butterflies*, a *pas de huit* choreographed by Nicolas Legat to the minuet in Mozart's *Don Giovanni*. They danced together for the last time on November 11, 1911, in *L'Oiseau d'Or*, a *pas de deux*, at the Royal Opera House, Covent Garden.

Chopiniana (page 86)

1 This was not the first time Pavlova had danced to Chopin's music. On September 22, 1902, to a piece orchestrated by Glazunov, Pavlova and Alfred Bekefi performed a *pas de deux* interpolated into Ivanov's ballet *Graziella*.
2 Because expenses for charity performances were kept to a minimum, most of the costumes were appropriated from the theater's wardrobe department. Those for the polonaise, for example, were from Petipa's disastrous *The Magic Mirror*, and for the *pas de deux* Obukhov wore a black velvet doublet from *The Fairy Doll*. Pavlova's costume, the only one for which a special provision had been made, was designed by Bakst and, according to her, was "an exact replica" of a costume worn by Taglioni. (Pavlova interview in the *Daily Mail*, London, July 21. 1909.)
3 On November 11, 1907. This dance was introduced into Pavlova's repertoire at the Palace Theatre, London, in 1912.
4 Akim Volynsky, quoted from Vera Krasovskaya, *Anna Pavlova* (Leningrad and Moscow: Iskusstvo, 1965).
5 Michel Fokine, *Fokine: Memoirs of a Ballet Master* (Boston and Toronto: Little, Brown, 1961).

The Swan (page 89)

1 Date established by Vera Krasovskaya and published in *Anna Pavlova* (Leningrad and Moscow: Iskusstvo, 1965). The occasion was a performance in aid of the charitable society of Her Imperial Highness Olga Alexandrovna, for newborn children and impoverished mothers at the Imperial Maternal Establishment. (Information supplied by Vera Krasovskaya.) On the same evening Karsavina performed Fokine's *Dance of the Fakirs*, set to Arensky's music. Some seventy years later, in conversation with the authors, she remembered the performance but not the date or location.
2 André Levinson, "Anna Pavlova," in *Solntse Rosii*, St. Petersburg, 1913, No. 1.
3 One of the greatest exponents of this genre was the brilliant actor N. Hodotov. His celebrated rendition of K. Balmont's poem "The Dying Swan," recited to musical accompaniment of Y. Vilbushevich, had been included in charity concerts in which Pavlova and Fokine had danced.
4 Pavlova's costume, designed by Bakst, was almost identical to the Maryinsky Odette costume. Bakst

also designed Karsavina's costume for *Dance of the Fakirs*.

5 Preobrajenskaya and Trefilova were the celebrated interpreters of this role during Pavlova's time, and later Karsavina, in 1908.

6 Vera Krasovskaya, *Anna Pavlova* (Leningrad and Moscow: Iskusstvo, 1965).

Swan Lake (page 92)

1 This was Pavlova's third independent tour at the head of a company. The first was to Moscow in the spring of 1907, the second to Riga in February 1908, when she was also partnered by Adolph Bolm.

2 *Die Post*, Berlin, June 1, 1908.

3 Ibid.

4 *Berliner Börsen-Courier*, May 8, 1909.

5 *Berliner Tageblatt*, May 8, 1909.

La Fille Mal Gardée (page 94)

1 Pavlova made her debut as Lise with Fokine as Colin at the Hermitage Theater, Moscow, on June 2, 1907.

Giselle (page 96)

1 *Berliner Zeitung am Mittag*, May 27, 1908.

2 *Illustrirtes Wiener Extrablatt*, May 28, 1909.

3 *Neues Wiener Tagblatt*, May 28, 1909.

4 *Paquita*, followed by *divertissements*.

Les Sylphides (page 98)

1 Diaghilev was almost preempted by Kchessinskaya. Two months after one of her (several) farewell benefits, the *Petersburgskii dnevik teatrala* of April 4, 1904, recorded that Kchessinskaya intended to visit Paris to negotiate a ballet season from May 15 to June 1 at the Théâtre Sarah Bernhardt, starring herself, with fifty dancers from the Maryinsky. The tour was obviously postponed—indefinitely. Diaghilev beat Kchessinskaya in the race to the Place du Châtelet.

2 French review quoted in *The Lady*, London, November 2, 1911.

3 *Le Figaro*, Paris, June 5, 1909.

4 S. L. Grigoriev, *The Diaghilev Ballet, 1909–1929* (London: Constable, 1953).

5 Michel Fokine, in *Novoe russkoe slovo*, New York; quoted in Victor Dandré, *Anna Pavlova in Art and Life* (London: Cassell, 1932).

Cléopâtre (page 101)

1 No photographs are known to exist of Pavlova as Veronica in *Egyptian Nights*. Charity performances were rarely, if ever, photographed.

2 Michel Fokine, *Fokine: Memoirs of a Ballet Master* (Boston and Toronto: Little, Brown, 1961).

3 *Comoedia*, Paris, June 5, 1909.

4 Fokine, *Fokine: Memoirs of a Ballet Master*.

5 Michel Fokine, "Michel Fokine Remembers," in *The Dance Magazine*, New York, August 1931.

6 Ibid.

7 Ibid. This ability was evident even in minor roles, which Pavlova always enjoyed playing. In 1911, at Covent Garden, for instance, she played Cleopatra's slave, the role Karsavina had created at the Paris premiere. Her performance in this tiny part did not go unnoticed. On October 30 a critic for the *Standard* stated an unequivocal opinion: "Mme. Pavlova proved that, apart from all the wealth of gesture and perfection of detail that belongs to the best among her colleagues, she is supreme as an actress."

Le Festin (page 102)

1 Neither Paris nor St. Petersburg would ever see Pavlova and Nijinsky together in *Giselle*. London was the only city accorded this privilege, during Diaghilev's 1911 fall season.

2 Upon her return to St. Petersburg Pavlova complained to the press that in Paris she had not been given an opportunity to perform her best roles. A surprising statement when one considers her professed allegiance to Fokine. But, then, Pavlova always wanted the best of both worlds.

Russian Dance (page 104)

1 The gala, in aid of the victims of the Midi earthquake, was organized by the Paris Press Syndicate.

2 Pavlova's performance at the Londesborough party on July 19, 1909, was her second appearance in London. Her first, hitherto generally unknown, took place a week earlier, on July 12, at a private party in the home of Mrs. Potter Palmer at Carlton House Terrace. There has previously been some confusion as to the exact date of the Londesborough party, because Pavlova described the event in a letter that she dated July 14, five days *before* the party was given. This letter, addressed to "Edward," is now in the Bibliothèque de l'Opéra, Paris, and the date has been verified by the authors. "Edward" was none other than Edward Faser, the impresario who had been responsible for Pavlova's first tours abroad and who hoped to organize a London season for her in 1910. It appears that Pavlova (who signed a lucrative contract with London impresario Daniel Mayer on July 20, the day after the Londesborough party) simply backdated her letter to Faser after she had obtained a better deal in London.

3 Pavlova always enjoyed performing for royalty. When the king asked her if she knew the popular dance the Paraguay, she performed it impromptu in her heavy *Russian Dance* costume.

Coppélia (page 107)

1 The occasion was a revival of the ballet, which had not been performed since the 1904–05 season. In two acts and three scenes, it was mounted by Ludovico Saracco, who also played Dr. Coppélius. The other parts were played by members of the resident Metropolitan Opera Ballet.
2 *New York Press*, March 1, 1910.
3 *New York Times*, March 1, 1910.
4 *Globe and Commercial Advertiser*, New York, March 1, 1910.
5 Ibid.
6 *Evening Mail*, New York, March 1, 1910.

Pas de Deux (page 109)

1 The performance was in aid of the pension and endowment fund of the Metropolitan. As well as *Pas de Deux*, Pavlova and Mordkin danced *Bacchanale*. The remainder of the program was devoted to opera: Act 1 of *Pagliacci*, Act 4 of *Il Trovatore*, Act 2 of *Tosca*, and Act 3 of *La Gioconda*, conducted by Toscanini, with the resident *corps de ballet* performing the Dance of the Hours. The *New York Times* noted on March 2, 1910, that "the total receipts were somewhere in the neighborhood of $15,000."
2 *New York Times*, March 2, 1910.
3 Ibid.
4 *The Times*, London, April 19, 1910.
5 *Pas de Deux* was sometimes given a more specific title. It was called *Visions* when it was performed at Mrs. Payne Whitney's private party on February 26, 1910, which marked Pavlova's American debut. Various other titles included *Bleichmann Adagio*, *Simple Aveu*, and *Danses Classiques*. The variety of titles was matched by the diversity of format. Music for the entrée, when there was one, and for the adagio was at first usually credited to Bleichmann. Some later playbills credit Thomé or Drigo as composer of the adagio. The variations for Pavlova and her partner could hardly have been more variable; composers credited include Tchaikovsky, Bartlett, Delibes, Glazunov, and Drigo. Bleichmann was occasionally named as composer of the coda. When choreographers were mentioned, Gorsky or Mordkin was usually named, and Schervachidze and Korovin were sometimes credited as costume designers. Probably because *Pas de Deux* was subject to such extreme change, composers, choreographers, and designers for the various dances were often not credited at all.

Valse Caprice (page 110)

1 At the benefit for Marie Petipa. The *pas de deux* was inserted into the ballet *Marquitantka (La Vivandière)*.

2 During Kchessinskaya's guest appearances in Vienna. The *pas de deux* was inserted into the ballet *Excelsior*.
3 *The Times*, London, April 19, 1910.
4 *Graphic*, London, April 30, 1910.
5 *Daily Telegraph*, London, April 19, 1910.
6 *Tatler*, London, April 27, 1910.
7 *Graphic*, London, May 28, 1910.

Bacchanale (page 114)

1 Four different bacchanales were direct predecessors of this *pas de deux*.

In Petipa's 1900 production of *The Seasons*, the bacchanale in the final scene was a *pas de crotales*, with the dancers' cymbals accompanying the frenzied measures of Glazunov's music for Autumn. The leading bacchantes in this refined revel, danced in strictly classical style, were Pavel Gerdt and Marie Petipa, who wore a traditional tutu elegantly festooned with vine leaves. Pavlova never danced in this bacchanale.

On January 28, 1907, a new production of *The Seasons* was premiered at the Maryinsky. As restaged by Nicolas Legat, the bacchanale, danced by Pavlova and Samuil Andrianov in free-flowing costumes designed by Golovin, was considerably less restrained than its predecessor. The ballet, which Svetlov considered "exquisitely vulgar," provoked a storm of protest from the audience.

Two years later, another ballet entitled *The Seasons* was given at the Maryinsky. For the ballet school's graduation performance on March 22, 1909, Fokine created a choreographic fantasy to music by Tchaikovsky. The highlight of this ballet was the bacchanale in the Autumn scene performed by the junior pupils. Several critics compared them to the pupils of Isadora Duncan, who had danced on the same stage the previous year.

A few months later, Fokine used Glazunov's Autumn music from *The Seasons* for a bacchanale incorporated into his production of *Cléopâtre*, given in Paris during Diaghilev's Saison Russe in May and June 1909. The bacchantes were clad in exotic Grecian costumes designed by Bakst. Vera Fokina and Sophia Fedorova led the frenzied bacchanalian revel—too frenzied, it seems, for St. Petersburg. Several prominent dancers, including Pavlova, thwarted Fokine's attempts to mount it at the Maryinsky the following autumn. It was finally premiered in St. Petersburg on January 22, 1910, at the Noblemen's Hall.

The bacchanale danced by Pavlova and Mordkin to Glazunov's Autumn music was the most frenzied of them all. This evocation of ancient Greece, though closer to Fokine than Petipa, was arranged by Mordkin. *The Times* thought it was "a triumph for the costumiers as well as for the dancers." Pavlova wore the costume Bakst had designed for her as Actea in *Eunice,* a cream silk chiton with red spots and border. Mordkin's costume (or lack of it) was by a designer unknown.

2 *Graphic,* London, May 28, 1910.
3 Conversation with Cyril Beaumont.
4 *The Times,* London, April 19, 1910.
5 *Daily Telegraph,* London, May 2, 1911.

Le Papillon (page 120)

1 During the course of Pavlova's career at least five other "butterfly" roles were included in her repertoire. (1) She first danced in *Caprices of the Butterfly,* a ballet choreographed by Petipa to music by Krotkov, at the Hermitage Theater, Moscow, in the spring of 1907. (2) *Pas des Papillons,* a *pas de deux* choreographed by Fokine to Chopin's "Minute Waltz," was performed by Pavlova and Fokine on November 11, 1907, and was later billed as *Le Papillon* when Pavlova and Mordkin danced it in New York in 1910 and as *Les Papillons* or *Papillons* when Pavlova and Novikoff danced it at the Palace Theatre, London, in 1912. (3) *Papillon,* a *pas de deux* choreographed by Nicolas Legat to music by Asafiev, was performed by Pavlova and Nijinsky on December 13, 1909. (4) *La Naissance du Papillon,* a *divertissement* to music by Delibes arranged by Pavlova for herself and seven of her pupils, was presented at the Palace Theatre in 1912. (5) *Japanese Butterfly,* a solo choreographed by Pavlova to Grieg's "Butterfly Dance," was first performed at the Royal Opera House, Covent Garden, on September 13, 1923.
2 The music, which in Pavlova's programs was often unidentified but was occasionally attributed to Drigo, is in fact by Minkus and is from *Roxana,* the four-act Petipa ballet first performed in 1878. By the turn of the century this ballet had disappeared from the Maryinsky repertoire. On January 20, 1902, Kchessinskaya introduced this variation

into Gorsky's production of *Don Quixote* at its St. Petersburg premiere.
3 *Los Angeles Examiner,* July 29, 1916.

L'Oiseau d'Or (page 123)

1 *Daily Mail,* London, November 4, 1911.
2 *Standard,* London, November 4, 1911.
3 Ibid.

La Rose Mourante (page 124)

1 As Dame Marie Rambert put it, "He wanted to direct her, and Pavlova would not be directed. . . . Diaghilev inspired in people a love of ballet and choreography, while Pavlova excited in people the desire to dance."
2 The London press reviews of Diaghilev's 1911 fall season testify to this.
3 Dame Ninette de Valois emphasized this aspect of Pavlova's art in a lecture to the Pavlova Society. "When I was young, dancing was divided into technique and virtuosity. Now it's all muddled up, and virtuosity, for some strange reason, is called technique. . . . It takes a great technique to do the simple things that Pavlova did. . . . People whirl today. Pavlova performed a pirouette. It may only have been two, but if you had ever seen it, you would never forget it."
4 Troy and Margaret West Kinney, *The Dance* (New York: Tudor, 1936).
5 Ibid.
6 This music has previously been confused with Tchaikovsky's "Valse Bluette" (op. 72, no. 11), which was orchestrated by Drigo and interpolated into the last act of *Swan Lake* in 1895.
7 The critic for the *Tatler* wrote on May 15, 1912, "If there is any criticism to make in a performance so absolutely lovely, it is that, until the last bar in which she suddenly collapses, the rose had never shown the very slightest evidence of dying, her demise thus coming upon us as quite a shock."

Bibliography

Books Devoted to Pavlova

Algeranoff, Harcourt. *My Years with Pavlova*. London: Heinemann, 1957. New York: British Book Service, 1957.

Amphlett, E. P. C. *Memorial to Pavlova*. London, 1945.

Beaumont, Cyril W. *Anna Pavlova*. 3d ed. London: Beaumont, 1945. First edition published in 1932.

Bie, Oscar; Paul Barchan; and Max Osborn. *Anna Pawlowa*. Berlin: Cassirer, 1913.

Cull, A. Tulloch. *Poems to Pavlova*. London: Jenkins, 1913.

Dandré, Victor. *Anna Pavlova in Art and Life*. London: Cassell, 1932. Reissued by Blom, New York, in 1970. Reprinted by Arno Press, New York, in 1979.

Franks, A. H., ed.; in collaboration with members of the Pavlova Commemoration Committee. *Pavlova: A Biography*. London: Burke, 1956. Reprinted by Da Capo Press, New York, in 1979. Published in Russian as *Anna Pavlova, 1881–1931* (translated by Y. Dobrovolskaya, edited by Elena Surits) by Izdatelstvo Inostrannoy Literatury, Moscow, in 1956.

Hyden, Walford. *Pavlova: The Genius of the Dance*. London: Constable, 1931.

Kerensky, Oleg. *Anna Pavlova*. London: Hamish Hamilton, 1973. New York: Dutton, 1973.

Krasovskaya, Vera. *Anna Pavlova*. Leningrad and Moscow: Iskusstvo, 1965.

Krauss, Ernst. *Anna Pavlova: Haar Leven en haar Kunst*. Amsterdam: Meulenhoff, 1931.

Levinson, André. *Anna Pavlova*. Paris: Grjébine & Vishgnak, 1928.

Lewalter, Ernst. *Unsterbliche Anna Pawlowa: Das Märchen ihres Lebens und ihrer Kunst*. Dresden: Reissner, 1938.

Magriel, Paul, ed. *Pavlova: An Illustrated Monograph*. New York: Holt, 1947. Reprinted in *Nijinsky, Pavlova, Duncan: Three Lives in Dance* by Da Capo Press, New York, in 1977.

Malvern, Gladys. *Dancing Star: The Story of Anna Pavlova*. New York: Messner, 1942. London and Glasgow: Collins, 1962.

May, Helen. *The Swan: The Story of Anna Pavlova*. Edinburgh and New York: Nelson, 1958.

Olivéroff, André; as told to John Gill. *Flight of the Swan: A Memory of Anna Pavlova*. New York: Dutton, 1932. Reprinted by Da Capo Press, New York, in 1979.

Oukrainsky, Serge. *My Two Years with Anna Pavlova*. Los Angeles: Suttonhouse, 1940.

Pavlova, Anna. *Tanzende Füsse: Der Weg meines Lebens*. With an introduction by Arthur Grunenberg. Dresden: Reissner, 1928. Reissued in 1931 without text as *Tänze von Anna Pawlowa im Bilde*.

Schmidt-Aleman, Heinz P. *Anna Pawlowa: Die Ballerina des Zaren*. Berlin: Deutsche Buchvertriebs und Verlags, 1952.

Stier, Theodore. *With Pavlova Round the World*. London: Hurst & Blackett, 1929.

Svetlov, Valerian. *Anna Pavlova*. Translated by A. Grey. Paris: Brunoff, 1922. Reprinted by Dover, New York, in 1974.

——— *Anna Pavlova*. London: British-Continental Press, 1931. A 32-page monograph.

Related Works

Amberg, George. *Ballet in America*. New York: Duell, Sloan & Pearce, 1949.

Astruc, Gabriel. *Le Pavillon des fantômes*. Paris: Grasset, 1929.

Aubel, Hermann and Marianne. *Der Künstlerische Tanz unserer Zeit*. Leipzig: Karl Robert Langewiesche, 1935.

Bakhrushin, Yuri. *Istoria russkogo baleta*. 2d ed. Moscow: Prosveshchenia, 1973. First edition published by Sovietskaya Rossia, Moscow, in 1965.

Baril, Jacques. *Dictionnaire de danse*. Paris: Editions du Seuil, 1964.

Beaton, Cecil. *Ballet*. London: Wingate, 1951. Garden City, N.Y.: Doubleday, 1951.

Beaumont, Cyril W. *Bookseller at the Ballet: Memoirs, 1891–1929*. London: Beaumont, 1975.

———— *The Complete Book of Ballets*. Rev. ed. London: Putnam, 1951.

———— *The Diaghilev Ballet in London*. London: Putnam, 1940.

———— *Enrico Cecchetti: A Memoir*. London: Beaumont, 1929.

———— *Five Centuries of Ballet Design*. London: Studio, 1939.

———— *Michel Fokine and His Ballets*. London: Beaumont, 1935.

Bedells, Phyllis. *My Dancing Days*. London: Phoenix House, 1954.

Benois, Alexandre. *Memoirs*. Vol. 2. Translated by Moura Budberg. London: Chatto & Windus, 1964.

———— *Reminiscences of the Russian Ballet*. Translated by Mary Britnieva. London: Putnam, 1941. Reprinted by Da Capo Press, New York, in 1977.

Buckle, Richard. *Diaghilev*. London: Weidenfeld & Nicolson, 1979. New York: Atheneum, 1979.

———— *Nijinsky*. London: Weidenfeld & Nicolson, 1971. New York: Simon & Schuster, 1971. Reissued in paperback by Penguin, London, and Avon, New York, in 1975. Reprinted, with revisions, by Penguin in 1980.

Chaplin, Charles. *My Autobiography*. London: Bodley Head, 1964. New York: Simon & Schuster, 1964.

Chiriaieff, Alexander. *Petersburgskii balet: Vospominanya*. Leningrad, 1941.

Chujoy, Anatole, and P. W. Manchester, eds. *The Dance Encyclopedia*. Rev. & enl. ed. New York: Simon & Schuster, 1967.

Chumakov, V. *O memyarach baletmeistera*. St. Petersburg, 1907.

Cowles, Virginia. *The Last Tsar and Tsarina*. London: Book Club Associates, by arrangement with Weidenfeld & Nicolson, 1977. New York: Putnam, 1977.

Crawford Flitch, J. E. *Modern Dancing and Dancers*. London: Grant Richards, 1912. Philadelphia: Lippincott, 1912.

de Valois, Dame Ninette. *Come Dance with Me: A Memoir, 1898–1956*. London: Hamish Hamilton, 1957. Cleveland: World, 1957.

Dobrovolskaya, Galina. M. *Fokine: Umirayushchi lebed*. Edited by Yuri Slonimsky. Leningrad: G.M.I., 1961.

Earley, Mary Dawn. *Stars of the Twenties Observed by James Abbe*. With an introduction by Lillian Gish. London: Thames & Hudson, 1975. New York: Viking, 1975.

Fokine, Michel. *Fokine: Memoirs of a Ballet Master*. Translated by Vitale Fokine, edited by Anatole Chujoy. Boston and Toronto: Little, Brown, 1961. London: Constable, 1961.

———— *Protiv techeniya*. Leningrad and Moscow: Iskusstvo, 1962.

Fülöp-Miller, René, and Joseph Gregor. *The Russian Theatre*. Translated by Paul England. London: Harrap, 1930.

Garling, Jean. *Australian Notes on the Ballet*. Sydney: Legend Press, n.d.

Genthe, Arnold. *As I Remember*. New York: Day, 1936.

———— *The Book of the Dance*. New York: Mitchell Kennerly, 1916.

Grigoriev, S. L. *The Diaghilev Ballet, 1909–1929*. Translated and edited by Vera Bowen. London: Constable, 1953. Reissued in paperback by Penguin, London and New York, in 1960.

Guest, Ivor, ed. *La Fille mal gardée*. Famous Ballets, vol. 1. London: Dancing Times, 1960.

Haskell, Arnold L. *Ballet Panorama*. 3d ed., rev. London: Batsford, 1948. First edition published in 1938.

———— *Balletomania: The Story of an Obsession*. London: Gollancz, 1934. Revised edition published as *Balletomania Then and Now* by Weidenfeld & Nicolson, London, and Knopf, New York, in 1977. Reprinted, with revisions, by Penguin in 1979.

———— *The Russian Genius in Ballet*. Oxford and New York: Pergamon, 1963.

Haskell, Arnold L., with Walter Nouvel. *Diaghileff: His Artistic and Private Life*. London: Gollancz, 1935. Reprinted by Da Capo Press, New York, in 1978.

Hoffman, Malvina. *A Sculptor's Odyssey*. London: Scribner, 1936.

Hurok, Sol. *S. Hurok Presents the World of Ballet*. London: Robert Hale, 1955.

Hurok, Sol, in collaboration with Ruth Goode. *Impresario*. London: Macdonald, 1947.

Ikonnikov. *Noblesse russe*. Paris, 1957.

Johnson, A. E. *The Russian Ballet*. London: Constable, 1913. Boston: Houghton Mifflin, 1913.

Karsavina, Tamara. *Theatre Street*. Rev. ed. London: Constable, 1948. New York: Dutton, 1961. First edition published by Heinneman, London, in 1930.

Kchessinskaya, Mathilde. *Dancing in Petersburg*. Translated by Arnold Haskell. London: Gollancz, 1960. Garden City, N.Y.: Doubleday, 1961.

Khudekov, Sergei. *Istoria tantsev*. Petrograd, 1917.

Kinney, Troy and Margaret West. *The Dance*. New York: Tudor, 1936.

Kochno, Boris. *Le Ballet*. Paris: Hachette, 1954.

———— *Diaghilev and the Ballets Russes*. Translated by Adrienne Foulke. New York: Harper & Row, 1970. London: Allen Lane, Penguin Press, 1971.

Koegler, Horst. *The Concise Oxford Dictionary of Ballet*. Oxford and New York: Oxford University Press, 1977.

Krasovskaya, Vera. *Nijinsky*. Translated by John E. Bowlt. New York: Schirmer, 1979.

———— *Russkii baletnyi teatr nachala XX veka*. Vol. 1: *Khoreografy*. Leningrad: Iskusstvo, 1971. Vol. 2: *Tantsovshchiki*. Leningrad: Iskusstvo, 1972.

———— *Russkii baletnyi teatr vtoroi poloviny XIX veka*. Leningrad and Moscow: Iskusstvo, 1963.

———— *Stati o balete*. Leningrad: Iskusstvo, 1967.

Kyasht, Lydia. *Romantic Recollections*. Edited by Erica Beale. London and New York: Brentano, 1929. Reprinted by Da Capo Press, New York, in 1978.

Lavery, Sir John. *The Life of a Painter*. London: Cassell, 1940.

Legat, Nicolas. *Ballet Russe: Memoirs of Nicolas Legat*. With a foreword by Sir Paul Dukes. London: Methuen, 1939.

——— *The Story of the Russian School*. Translated and with a foreword by Sir Paul Dukes. London: British-Continental Press, 1932.

Leningrad State Theater Museum, ed. *Marius Petipa: Materiali, vospominanya, stati*. Leningrad: Iskusstvo, 1971.

Leshkov, D. I. *Marius Petipa, 1822–1910*. Petrograd, 1922.

Levinson, André. *La Danse d'aujourd'hui*. Duchârtre & Van Buggenhoudt, 1929.

——— *Staryi i novyi balet*. Petrograd: Svobodnoye Iskusstvo, 1918.

——— *Les Visages de la danse*. Paris: Grasset, 1933.

Lieven, Prince Peter. *The Birth of Ballets-Russes*. Translated by L. Zarine. London: Allen & Unwin, 1936. Reprinted by Dover, New York, in 1973.

Lifar, Serge. *A History of Russian Ballet*. Translated by Arnold Haskell. London: Hutchinson, 1954.

——— *Serge Diaghilev: His Life, His Work, His Legend; An Intimate Biography*. London and New York: Putnam, 1940. Reprinted by Da Capo Press, New York, in 1976.

——— *The Three Graces*. Translated by Gerard Hopkins. London: Cassell, 1959.

Lopukhov, Fëdor. *Puti baletmeistera*. Berlin: Petropolis, 1925.

Macdonald, Nesta. *Diaghilev Observed*. New York: Dance Horizons, 1975. London: Dance Books, 1975.

Moore, Lillian. *Artists of the Dance*. New York: Crowell, 1938.

Nikitina, Alice. *Nikitina*. Translated by Moura Budberg. London: Wingate, 1959. Toronto: Smithers, 1959.

Pask, Edward H. *Enter the Colonies, Dancing*. Melbourne: Oxford University Press, 1979.

Pleshcheyev, Alexander. *M. I. Petipa, 1847–1907*. St. Petersburg, 1907.

——— *Moye vremya*. Paris: Editeurs Réunis, 1939.

——— *Nash balet*. St. Petersburg, 1899.

——— *Pod seniyou kulis*. Paris: Livre Etranger, 1936.

Propert, W. A. *The Russian Ballet in Western Europe, 1909–1920*. London: Bodley Head, 1921.

Prouzhan, I. N. *Bakst*. Leningrad: Iskusstvo, 1975.

Racster, Olga. *The Master of the Russian Ballet: The Memoirs of Cav. Enrico Cecchetti*. With an introduction by Anna Pavlova. London: Hutchinson, 1922. Reprinted by Da Capo Press, New York, in 1978.

Rambert, Dame Marie. *Quicksilver: The Autobiography of Marie Rambert*. London: Macmillan, 1972. New York: St. Martin's Press, 1972.

Rebling, Eberhard. *Ballett Gestern und Heute*. Berlin: Henschelverlag Kunst, 1957.

Ricketts, Charles. *Self-Portrait*. London: Peter Davies, 1939.

Roslavleva, Natalia. *Era of the Russian Ballet, 1770–1965*. London: Gollancz, 1966. New York: Dutton, 1966. Reprinted by Da Capo Press, New York, in 1979.

Schneider, Ilya. *Isadora Duncan: The Russian Years*. London: Macdonald, 1968. New York: Harcourt, Brace & World, 1969.

Seton-Watson, Hugh. *The Decline of Imperial Russia, 1855–1914*. London: Methuen, 1952.

Slonimsky, Yuri. *Mastera baleta*. Leningrad: Iskusstvo, 1937.

——— *P. I. Tchaikovsky: Baletnyi teatr ego vremeni*. Moscow, 1956.

Slonimsky, Yuri, ed. *Tshchetnaya predostorozhnost*. Leningrad, 1961.

Smith, Eleanor. *Life's a Circus*. London: Longmans, Green, 1939.

Sokolova, Lydia. *Dancing for Diaghilev*. Edited by Richard Buckle. London: Murray, 1960.

Solyannikov, Nikolai. *Vospominanya*. Moscow: V.T.O., n.d.

Stravinsky, Igor. *An Autobiography*. New York: Norton, 1962.

Svetlov, Valerian. *Sovremenni balet*. St. Petersburg, 1911.

——— *Terpsichore*. St. Petersburg, 1906.

——— *Thamar Karsavina*. Edited by Cyril W. Beaumont. London: Beaumont, 1922.

Teliakovsky, Vladimir. *Vospominanya*. Leningrad and Moscow: Iskusstvo, 1965.

Tikhomirov, Vasily. *Artyst, baletmeister, pedagog*. Moscow: Iskusstvo, 1971.

Vaillat, Léandre. *Histoire de la danse*. Paris: Plon, 1942.

Vazem, Ekaterina. *Zapiski balerini St. Petersburgskogo Bolshogo Teatra*. Leningrad and Moscow: Iskusstvo, 1937.

Volynsky, Akim. *Kniga likovanii*. Leningrad: Khoreografichesky Technicum, 1925. Translated by Seymour Bronsky as "The Book of Exultation," published in *Dance Scope*, Spring 1971, pp. 16–35, and continued in subsequent issues.

Wilson, G. B. L. *A Dictionary of Ballet*. New, enl. ed. London: A. & C. Black, 1974.

Yezhegodnik imperatorskikh teatrov (Annual of the Imperial Theaters), 1898–1914. St. Petersburg: Office of the Imperial Theaters.

Note

This bibliography lists books we have used as research sources. We have not attempted to list the thousands of articles about Pavlova that were published in the world press and that are available in special archives. The specialist in dance history is referred particularly to the articles cited in the notes (see pages 206–213) and is directed generally to the archives, periodicals, and newspapers cited throughout.

Repertoire

Entries are chronological by date of Pavlova's first performance. An asterisk indicates an uncertain date. Excerpts from familiar ballets that Pavlova retitled and performed as *divertissements* are not listed. Solos, *pas de deux,* and other *divertissements* are printed in italics. A double asterisk indicates an unknown choreographer.

	BALLET / DIVERTISSEMENT	DANCE / ROLE	COMPOSER	CHOREOGRAPHER
1892	The Magic Fairy Tale	Ballabile	Richter	Petipa
1897	Thetis and Peleus	Waterlily	Minkus, Delibes	Petipa
1898	Raymonda	Pas d'ensemble	Glazunov	Petipa
	The Two Stars	Star	Pugni	Petipa
	Daughter of the Pharaoh	Pas de trois	Pugni	Petipa
1899	The Halt of the Cavalry	Pas de quatre	Armsheimer	Petipa
	The Imaginary Dryads	Daughter of the Count	Pugni	Gerdt
		Interpolated variation from *The Vestal Virgin*	M. Ivanov	Petipa
	Clorinda	Variation	Keller	Gorsky
	La Fille Mal Gardée	Pas de six	Hertel	Dauberval/Petipa, Ivanov
	La Fille Mal Gardée	Pas de trois	Hertel	Dauberval/Petipa, Ivanov
	Giselle	Zulme	Adam	Coralli, Perrot/Petipa
	The Sleeping Beauty	Fairy Candide	Tchaikovsky	Petipa
	Esmeralda	Friend of Fleur de Lys	Pugni	Perrot/Petipa
	Marcobomba	Polka Folichonne	Pugni	Perrot/Ivanov
1900	The Pearl	Dance of the Pearls	Drigo	Petipa
	The Seasons (Les Saisons)	Hoarfrost	Glazunov	Petipa
	Harlequinade (Les Millions d'Arlequin)	La Sérénade, Le Rendezvous des Amoureux, La Polonaise, La Réconciliation, & Pas d'ensemble	Drigo	Petipa
	The Awakening of Flora	Aurora	Drigo	Petipa, Ivanov
	Bluebeard	Anna	Schenck	Petipa
	The Awakening of Flora	Flora	Drigo	Petipa, Ivanov
	Bluebeard	Venus	Schenck	Petipa
	King Candaule	Diana	Pugni	Petipa
	La Bayadère	Shade	Minkus	Petipa
1901	Camargo	Snow	Minkus	Petipa
		Pas de trois	Wrangel	Petipa
	Marquitantka (La Vivandière)	Pas de six	Pugni	Saint-Léon/Petipa
	Parisian Bazaar (Le Marché des Innocents)	Lisette	Pugni	Petipa
	Raymonda	Henrietta	Glazunov	Petipa
	Marquitantka (La Vivandière)	Katya	Pugni	Saint-Léon/Petipa
	Paquita	Pas de trois	Minkus	Petipa
	Paquita	Grand pas variation	Minkus	Petipa

	BALLET / DIVERTISSEMENT	DANCE / ROLE	COMPOSER	CHOREOGRAPHER
1901	Sylvia	Queen of the Naiads	Delibes	Ivanov, Gerdt
	The Sleeping Beauty	Florine	Tchaikovsky	Petipa
	The Magic Flute	Lise	Drigo	Ivanov
	The Nutcracker	Golden Waltz	Tchaikovsky	Ivanov
1902	Don Quixote	Juanita	Minkus, Drigo	Petipa, Gorsky
		Fandango	Napravnik	Petipa, Gorsky
	Harlequinade	Pierrette	Drigo	Petipa
	Javotte	Pas d'ensemble	Saint-Saëns	Mariquita / Gerdt
	La Bayadère	Nikiya	Minkus	Petipa
	*Coppélia	Friend of Swanilda	Delibes	Saint-Léon / Petipa
	The Humpbacked Horse	Nereid	Pugni	Saint-Léon / Petipa
	Swan Lake	Spanish Dance	Tchaikovsky	Petipa
	Graziella	Interpolated pas de deux	Chopin	**
	Le Corsaire	Pas d'esclave	Oldenbourg	Petipa
	Le Corsaire	Gulnare	Adam, Pugni, Delibes	Mazilier / Petipa
	The Humpbacked Horse	Dance of the Ural Cossacks	Pugni	Saint-Léon / Petipa
	Le Corsaire	Pas de trois	Adam, Pugni, Delibes	Mazilier / Petipa
	La Source	Ephemerida	Delibes, Minkus	Saint-Léon / Coppini
1903	The Fairy Doll	Spanish Doll	Bayer, Rubinstein, et al.	N. & S. Legat
	The Magic Mirror	Pas de trois suisse	Koreshchenko	Petipa
	The Sleeping Beauty	Canary Fairy	Tchaikovsky	Petipa
	Giselle	Giselle	Adam	Coralli, Perrot / Petipa
	Daughter of the Pharaoh	Ramsea	Pugni	Petipa
	The Naiad and the Fisherman	Naiad	Pugni	Perrot / Petipa
1904	Paquita	Paquita	Deldevez, Minkus	Mazilier / Petipa
	Le Corsaire	Medora	Adam, Pugni, Delibes	Mazilier / Petipa
	At the Crossroads	Carmen	Armsheimer	Chiriaieff
1905	Daughter of the Pharaoh	Grand pas de crotales	Pugni	Petipa
	Midsummer Night's Dream	Elemental	Mendelssohn-Bartholdy, Minkus	Petipa
	Don Quixote	Kitri	Minkus, Drigo	Petipa, Gorsky
	The Talisman	Bayadère	Drigo	Petipa
	The Enchanted Forest	Ilka	Drigo	Ivanov
1906	Daughter of the Pharoah	Bint-Anta	Pugni et al.	Petipa, Gorsky
	Daughter of the Pharoah	Aspicia	Pugni	Petipa
	The Vine	Vine Spirit	Rubinstein	Fokine
	Raymonda	Panaderos	Glazunov	Petipa
1907	Fiametta	Cupid	Minkus	Saint-Léon / Petipa
	The Seasons	Bacchanale	Glazunov	N. Legat
	Chopiniana (first version)	Pas de deux	Chopin	Fokine
	Eunice	Actea	Shcherbachev	Fokine
	The Halt of the Cavalry	Theresa	Armsheimer	Petipa
	The Animated Gobelin	Armida	N. Tcherepnin	Fokine
	La Fille Mal Gardée	Lise	Hertel	Dauberval / Petipa, Ivanov
	Coppélia	Swanilda	Delibes	Saint-Léon / Petipa
	Caprices of the Butterfly	Butterfly	Krotkov	Petipa
	Don Quixote	Street Dancer & Mercedes	Minkus	Petipa, Gorksy
	Pas des Papillons	————	Chopin	Fokine
	Le Pavillon d'Armide (first version)	Armida	N. Tcherepnin	Fokine
	The Purple Flower	Annunciata	Hartmann	N. Legat
	The Swan	————	Saint-Saëns	Fokine

	BALLET / DIVERTISSEMENT	DANCE / ROLE	COMPOSER	CHOREOGRAPHER
1908	The Sleeping Beauty	Aurora	Tchaikovsky	Petipa
	Eunice	Eunice	Shcherbachev	Fokine
	The Sleeping Beauty	Lilac Fairy	Tchaikovsky	Petipa
	Egyptian Nights	Veronica	Arensky	Fokine
	Chopiniana (second version)	Sylphide	Chopin	Fokine
	Swan Lake	Odette	Tchaikovsky	Ivanov
	Harlequinade	Columbine	Drigo	Petipa
1909	Swan Lake	Odette–Odile	Tchaikovsky	Petipa, Ivanov
	Night	——————	Rubinstein	N. Legat
	Les Sylphides	Sylphide	Chopin	Fokine
	Cléopâtre	Ta-Hor	Arensky et al.	Fokine
	Le Pavillon d'Armide (revised version)	Armida	N. Tcherepnin	Fokine
	Le Festin	Pas de deux	Bleichmann, Bartlett	Gorsky
	*Bacchanale	——————	Glazunov	Mordkin
	Russian Dance	——————	Tchaikovsky, Alabiev	Mordkin
	King Candaule	Nisia	Pugni	Petipa
	The Fairy Doll	Baby Doll	Bayer, Rubinstein, et al.	N. & S. Legat
	The Nutcracker	Spanish Dance	Tchaikovsky	Ivanov
	Papillon	——————	Asafiev	N. Legat
1910	Coppélia	Swanilda	Delibes	Saint-Léon / Saracco
	Valse Caprice	——————	Rubinstein	N. Legat
	Le Papillon	——————	Minkus	Pavlova
	The Legend of Azyiade (The Arabian Nights)	Azyiade	Rimsky-Korsakov et al.	Mordkin
	Giselle	Giselle	Adam	Gorsky / Mordkin
	Danse Orientale	——————	Arends, Rubinstein	Mordkin
	Danse Russe	——————	Giraud, M. Ivanov	**
	La Rose Mourante	——————	Drigo	Pavlova
1911	*Danse Espagnole*	——————	Rubinstein	Petipa
	Danse Hongroise	——————	Brahms	**
	Blue Danube	——————	Strauss	Pavlova
	Snowflakes (first version)	Snowflake	Tchaikovsky	Pavlova
	Cléopâtre	Slave	Arensky et al.	Fokine
	Giselle	Giselle	Adam	Ballets Russes production
	L'Oiseau d'Or	——————	Tchaikovsky	Petipa
	Le Carnaval	Columbine	Schumann	Fokine
	Variations	——————	Chopin	Fokine
	Souvenir d'Espagna	——————	Gillet	Chiriaieff
1912	*Coquetterie de Colombine*	——————	Drigo	N. & S. Legat
	Grand Pas Classique (Paquita) (first version)	Paquita	Minkus	Petipa / Chiriaieff, Cecchetti
	Amarilla	Amarilla	Glazunov et al.	Zajlich
	En Orange	——————	Giraud	Gorsky
	La Fille Mal Gardée (first version)	Eliza	Hertel	Petipa, Ivanov / Zajlich, Chiriaieff
	La Naissance du Papillon	Butterfly	Delibes	Pavlova
	Seven Daughters of the Mountain King	Crystal-Clear Spring	Spendiarov	Fokine
1913	Les Préludes	Sprit of Love	Liszt	Fokine
	Invitation to the Dance	Debutante	Weber	Zajlich
	*Coppélia	Swanilda	Delibes	Saint-Léon / Petipa / Clustine
	Giselle	Giselle	Adam	Petipa / Pavlova, Clustine

	BALLET / DIVERTISSEMENT	DANCE / ROLE	COMPOSER	CHOREOGRAPHER
(1913)	Pas de Trois	——————	Godard	Clustine
	The Magic Flute	Lise	Drigo	Ivanov / Pavlova, Cecchetti
	Oriental Fantasy	Oriental Enchantress	Serov, Mussorgsky,	
	(L'Orientale)		et al.	Zajlich
	Chopiniana	Sylphide	Chopin	Fokine / Clustine
	(Une Soirée de Chopin)			
	(Une Soirée de Danse)			
	The Halt of the Cavalry	Theresa	Armsheimer	Petipa / Zajlich, Cecchetti
	Gavotte	——————	Lincke	Clustine
1914	Egyptian Pas de Deux	——————	Arensky	Fokine / Clustine
	Danse Rustique	——————	Arends	Clustine
	Scène Dansante	——————	Boccherini	Clustine
	Anitra's Dance	——————	Grieg	Clustine
	Petite Danse Russe	——————	Dvořák	Clustine
	The Awakening of Flora	Flora	Drigo	Petipa, Ivanov / Clustine
	New Gavotte Pavlova	——————	Jacoby	Clustine
	Czarina Waltz	——————	Ackley, Auracher	Clustine
	The Pavlovana	——————	Moore	Clustine
	Minuet	——————	Mozart	Clustine
	The Fairy Doll	Fairy Doll	Bayer, Rubinstein,	
			et al.	N. & S. Legat / Clustine
1915	Raymonda	Raymonda	Glazunov	Petipa / Clustine
	Dragonfly	——————	Kreisler	Pavlova
	Russian Dance	——————	Kalinnikov	Clustine
	Snowflakes (second version)	Queen of the Snow	Tchaikovsky	Clustine
	Spanish Dances	Spanish Girl	Massenet,	
			Glazunov,	
			Moskowski	Clustine
1916	*Californian Poppy	——————	Tchaikovsky	Pavlova
	The Sleeping Beauty	Aurora	Tchaikovsky	Petipa / Clustine
	*Rondo	——————	Beethoven,	
			Kreisler	Pavlova
	Waltz	——————	Sousa	Clustine
1917	La Péri	Péri	Dukas	Stowitts, Clustine
	*Visions	Aurora	Tchaikovsky	Petipa / Clustine
	Assyrian Dance	——————	Saint-Saëns	Clustine
	Egyptian Ballet	Priestess	Luigini, Verdi,	
			et al.	Clustine
	Noir et Blanc	Mischievous Student	Chaminade	Clustine
	Valse Triste	——————	Sibelius	Clustine
	*The Enchanted Lake	Queen of the Lake	Schubert	Clustine
	(Schubertiana)			
1918	*Fairy Tales	Aurora	Tchaikovsky	Petipa / Clustine
	Danse des Fleurs	Naila	Delibes	Saint-Léon / Clustine
	The Last Song	Fiancée	Maurage	Clustine
	Minuet	——————	Marinuzzi	Clustine
	La Danse	——————	Kreisler	Pavlova
1919	*Mexican Dances	Mexican Girl	Padilla	Traditional
	*Autumn Leaves	Chrysanthemum	Chopin	Pavlova
	Pierrot	——————	Dvořák	Clustine
	Serenade	——————	Drigo	N. & S. Legat / Clustine
	*The Lorelei	Lorelei	Catalani	Clustine
	(The Ondines)			
1920	Three Wooden Dolls	Young Girl	Maurice-Lévy	Pavlova
	*Christmas	——————	Tchaikovsky	Pavlova, Clustine,
				Volinine
	Tambourine	——————	Rameau	Fokine / Clustine

	BALLET / DIVERTISSEMENT	DANCE / ROLE	COMPOSER	CHOREOGRAPHER
(1920)	*Minuet*	——————	Massenet	Clustine
	Pavlova Polka	——————	de Markoff	**
1921	The Fauns	Bacchante	Satz	Clustine
	Russian Dance	——————	Tchaikovsky	Clustine
	Dionysus	High Priestess	N. Tcherepnin	Clustine
	A Polish Wedding	Janka	Krupinski	Pianowski
1923	Ajanta's Frescoes	Oriental Maiden	A. Tcherepnin	Clustine
	(Ajanta Frescoes)			
	(Ajanta)			
	Oriental Impressions			
	Japanese Dances	Japanese Girl	Geehl	Fijima, Fumi
	Krishna and Radha	Radha	Banerji	Shankar
	Japanese Butterfly	——————	Grieg	Pavlova
	An Old Russian Folk Lore	Enchanted Bird-Princess	N. Tcherepnin	Novikoff
	(Russian Folk Lore)			
	(Russian Fairytale)			
	La Fille Mal Gardée	Lise	Hertel	Petipa, Ivanov /
	(second version)			Zajlich, Chiriaieff
1924	Don Quixote	Kitri	Minkus, Drigo	Gorsky, Novikoff
1925	The Romance of a Mummy	Priestess Isimkhab	N. Tcherepnin	Clustine
1926	*Masquerade*	——————	Wurmser	Pavlova
1927	*Au Bal*	——————	Tchaikovsky	Romanov
	Grand Pas Hongrois (Raymonda)	Raymonda	Glazunov	Petipa / Novikoff
	The Champions	——————	Hyden	Romanov
1928	*Polka Incroyable*	——————	Hyden	Clustine
	Grand Pas Classique (Paquita)	Paquita	Minkus	Petipa / Romanov
	(second version)			

OPERAS

	OPERA	DANCE / ROLE	COMPOSER	CHOREOGRAPHER
Maryinsky Theater, 1899–1910	The Demon	Lezghinka	Rubinstein	Petipa
	Carmen	Olé	Bizet	Petipa
	Der Freischütz	Waltz	Weber	**
	A Life for the Tsar	Polonaise & Mazurka	Glinka	Petipa
	Russlan and Ludmilla	Lezghinka	Glinka	Petipa
	Russalka	Gypsy dances	Dargomyzhsky	Petipa
	Don Giovanni	Pas de huit	Mozart	N. Legat
	Faust	Helen of Troy	Gounod	Petipa
	Carmen	Fandango	Bizet	N. Legat
World Tours, 1910–1930	Faust	Helen of Troy	Gounod	Clustine
	La Gioconda	Dance of the Hours	Ponchielli	Clustine
	Thais	Thais	Massenet	Clustine
	Orpheus	Shadow	Gluck	Clustine
	Romeo and Juliet	Queen of Spring	Gounod	Clustine
	The Dumb Girl of Portici	Fenella	Auber	——————
	Carmen	Entr'acte & Olé	Bizet	Clustine
	Aida	Priestess	Verdi	Clustine
	La Angelical Manuelita	Minuet	Mansilla	Clustine
	Mefistofele	Nymph	Boïto	Clustine
	Guarani	Indian woman	Gomez	Clustine

Index

Photo Credits